MAMMALS
OF THE SMOKIES

WRITTEN BY
EDWARD PIVORUN, MICHAEL HARVEY,
FRANK T. VAN MANEN, MICHAEL PELTON, JOSEPH CLARK,
KIM DELOZIER, AND BILL STIVER

GREAT SMOKY MOUNTAINS
ASSOCIATION
Gatlinburg, Tennessee

EDITED BY: Steve Kemp and Kent Cave
SERIES DESIGN BY: Christina Watkins
PRODUCTION BY: Lisa Horstman
EDITORIAL REVIEW & ASSISTANCE BY: Julie Brown, Caitlin Miller
COVER PHOTOGRAPH BY: Bill Lea

PRINTED IN HONG KONG

1 2 3 4 5 6 7 8 9

ISBN 978-0-937207-58-1

Published by Great Smoky Mountains Association.

Great Smoky Mountains Association is a nonprofit organization which supports the educational, scientific, and historical programs of Great Smoky Mountains National Park. Our publications are an educational service intended to enhance the public's understanding and enjoyment of the national park. If you would like to know more about our publications, memberships, and projects, please contact: Great Smoky Mountains Association, 115 Park Headquarters Road, Gatlinburg, TN 37738 (865) 436-7318. www.SmokiesInformation.org

This book is dedicated to
the scores of graduate students, professors, wildlife biologists, SCAs, volunteers, and others who have spent long wet days and shivering nights in the field gaining the knowledge we can now all proudly share.

CONTENTS

INTRODUCTION

Great Smoky Mountains National Park is well known for its tremendous diversity of species, and mammals are no exception. The first scientists to conduct a comprehensive survey of mammals in the newly established national park were two brothers, Edwin and Roy Komarek. Their study was published in 1938 by the Chicago Academy of Sciences and represents a valuable historic account of mammals during the time of transition to national park establishment. No such comprehensive survey has been conducted since. With the exception of white-tailed deer, elk, several carnivores, and a few bats and rodents, surprisingly few mammals have been studied extensively in the national park. Some of the reasons are that most mammals are very secretive and shy, are primarily active at night, and occur at relatively low densities, all of which complicates research. Yet, as you will discover from this book, many of these mammals are fascinating and have intriguing life histories.

With 65 species, the assemblage of mammals that occur in Great Smoky Mountains National Park is one of the most diverse in North America. One of the main reasons for this diversity is the wide range of elevations, from 874 feet at Abrams Creek to 6,643 feet at Clingmans Dome. At elevations above 3,000 feet, visitors may encounter mammals that are typically considered northern species, such as the red squirrel, Carolina northern flying squirrel, and rock vole. Below that elevation, you are more likely to encounter mammals whose distributions are centered in the Southern states, such as the golden mouse, Eastern harvest mouse, or marsh rice rat. Although the mammals that occur in the national park are diverse, most species have distributions that extend well beyond its boundaries into lower elevations. Notable exceptions are the Appalachian cottontail rabbit, rock vole, smoky shrew, and woodland jumping mouse, whose distributions are restricted. These follow the Appalachian Mountain chain north into southern Canada.

Small mammal species are the most numerous and include the shrews (Soricidae family, 8 species), bats (Vespertilionidae family, 11 species), and native rats and mice (Muridae (Cricetidae) family, 14 species). These mammals are not easily observed and are not considered as charismatic as black bears, white-tailed deer, or elk. But many of the small mammals play important roles within the ecosystem. Deer mice, for example, occur in these rich ecosystems at much greater densities than bears and their sheer numbers make them major competitors for important wildlife foods such as acorns.

WILDLIFE WATCHING

Observing mammals is probably one of the most challenging nature activities one can undertake, but also one of the most satisfying. Mammal sightings tend to occur by chance and one usually cannot expect to go to a certain area to observe specific species. The notable exceptions are white-tailed deer and coyotes in areas like Cades Cove, and elk in Cataloochee Valley. With the information in this book, however, you can learn more about the other mammals, their habits, and the areas in which they typically are found. Because mammals tend to be secretive and shy, they are often best observed from a distance, particularly in areas with little or no forest cover. Fields or open areas around historic buildings and settlements provide some of the best viewing areas for a wide array of mammals. The edge habitats where forests and fields meet are preferred by many small rodents, which, in turn, attract predators such as foxes, skunks, and raccoons. The open woodlands of the high elevations provide good opportunities to observe several smaller mammals, such as the red squirrel and the boreal red-backed mouse. Within the more densely forested areas common to much of the national park, mammal encounters become more and more accidental. Crossing paths with a hairy-tailed mole digging its way up through the soil or catching a glimpse of a weasel scampering behind a rock are rare occurrences, and one cannot plan for such observations other than covering many miles on backcountry trails.

The time of observation is also very important. White-tailed deer, squirrels, chipmunks, woodchucks, beavers, and river otters, for example, are best observed during the day. Other species, such as elk, are best observed during early morning and late evening. Elk also may be active on cloudy summer days and before or after storms. However, most mammals are nocturnal and you may only occasionally catch a glimpse of them while driving park roads at night. Evening and nighttime strolls along gated roads can result in exciting observations of bats, particularly if the road is near a stream, or of a raccoon shuffling from one feeding spot to the next. In some instances, your only evidence may be based on sounds, the yipping howl of coyotes or the high-pitched "cheeps" of southern flying squirrels right after sunset.

No special equipment is necessary to observe most mammals. Binoculars or a spotting scope can be useful to observe medium to large mammals, especially in open areas like Cades Cove. Binoculars occasionally are useful to observe smaller mammals from a distance. However, many mammal observations tend to be sudden, short encounters and often do not allow enough time to use binoculars. Bats are one of the exceptions in terms of observation equipment. There are devices available that can detect the high-frequency sounds emitted by bats during their activities. Different species use different approaches to echolocation and have distinct call signatures, which can be used for species identification. However, identification is not always 100% accurate and requires extensive training and advanced equipment and software.

Although observing mammals directly is challenging, they fortunately leave prominent signs wherever they go. Scats (droppings) are easily observed for a wide array of mammals, ranging from rabbits and deer to wild hogs and black bears. Scats of carnivores are particularly common and relatively easy to identify. Tracks also provide important clues to mammal presence and are particularly intriguing after snowfall. Observe how an otter has used the accumulated snow to slide into a river, follow the tracks of a coyote for miles along a hiking trail, and notice how squirrels and mice often use logs along their travel paths. The dens and burrows of mammals like the woodchuck and red fox (who often enlarge old woodchuck burrows) are easily recognized. Finally, you may occasionally find a dead animal or a carcass. Some shrews and moles produce a strong, musky odor that may have an unpleasant taste, so it is not uncommon to find them on hiking trails after being abandoned by predators. For most other species, only skeletal remains may be found of which the skull would give you the best chance of correct identification.

DANGEROUS WILDLIFE

Encounters with any of the mammals in the national park are exciting and visitors should feel encouraged to enjoy them. However, there are two major human safety considerations with regard to mammals.

First, several of the larger mammals can do physical harm when confronted. As the largest carnivore in the national park, the black bear can be potentially dangerous when encountered. Although black bears are very shy and secretive and will usually turn away from people, their behavior is sometimes unpredictable. Attacks on humans have occurred, inflicting serious injuries and death. Treat bear encounters with extreme caution and follow these guidelines. If you see a bear, remain watchful. Do not approach it. If your presence causes the bear to change its behavior (stops feeding, changes its travel direction, watches you), you are too close. Being too close may promote aggressive behavior from the bear such as running toward you, making loud noises, or swatting the ground. The bear is demanding more space. Do not run, but slowly back away, watching the bear. Try to increase the distance between you and the bear. If a bear persistently follows or approaches you, without vocalizing, or paw swatting, try changing your direction. If the bear continues to follow you, stand your ground. If the bear gets closer, talk loudly or shout. Act aggressively and try to intimidate the bear. Act together as a group if you have companions. Make yourselves look as large as possible (for example, show your backpack to look bigger). Throw non-food objects like small rocks at the bear. Gather a stout stick as a possible deterrent. Do not run or turn away from the bear. Do not leave food for the bear; this only encourages further problems.

Most injuries from black bear attacks are minor and result from a bear attempting to get to people's food. If the bear's behavior indicates that it is after your food and you are physically attacked, separate yourself from the food and slowly back away. However, if the bear shows no interest in your food and you are physically attacked, fight back aggressively with any available object. The bear may consider you prey! Help protect others by immediately reporting all bear incidents to a park ranger. Above all, keep your distance from bears.

Because of their size, elk probably are the second most dangerous animals in the national park. Especially during the fall rutting season, bull elk can become dangerous when approached by people. This is also true of white-tailed deer bucks. Always keep a safe distance from these animals, particularly during the rutting season. If an animal changes its behavior (runs or walks away) when you approach, you are too close. Park regulations state: *Willfully approaching within 50 yards or any distance that disturbs or displaces bear or elk is prohibited.*

Diseases are the second safety concern for people. Of all diseases common to mammals, rabies is by far the most serious threat. Rabies has been documented in Great Smoky Mountains National Park only in bats. Rabid bats are rarely aggressive. Although rabies has been found in many species of bats, its occurrence is relatively uncommon. However, because bats can carry and transmit rabies, they should not be handled. If you find a bat on the ground, do not pick it up.

Hanta pulmonary syndrome (HPS) is a potentially dangerous disease contracted from contact with the urine or feces of infected rodents such as the deer mouse. Avoid stirring up dust and dirt in which rodents have urinated or defecated.

RARE AND ENDANGERED MAMMALS . . . .

Sightings of mammals such as bobcats or black bears tend to be uncommon, so we often think of those animals as rare species. However, they are relatively common compared with a number of other mammals that are rarely seen or recorded. These rare species are nonetheless some of the most charming and charismatic mammals of the Great Smoky Mountains, including the long-tailed weasel, eastern spotted skunk, Allegheny woodrat, meadow jumping mouse, and rock vole. Several of these species have naturally low densities (long-tailed weasel, eastern spotted skunk) or may be limited by the amount of good habitat

(Allegheny woodrat occurs only at lower elevations), whereas others may be relatively abundant but only in localized populations (rock vole at higher elevations).

Two mammals are listed as federally endangered under the U.S. Endangered Species Act of 1973. The Carolina northern flying squirrel is an endangered subspecies whose distribution is limited to five isolated populations in western North Carolina and eastern Tennessee, including one in Great Smoky Mountains National Park. The northern flying squirrel is adapted to cold, boreal conditions, and its isolated populations may be considered a relict from the last ice age. They occur in the transition zone between coniferous forest, where they feed, and northern hardwood forests, which are needed for nesting sites. Human disturbance and habitat changes are the primary threats to this subspecies. More information on the distribution and abundance of the isolated populations is needed to better protect this unique mammal. The second endangered mammal is the Indiana bat. Indiana bat populations have declined drastically during the past 40 years. Human disturbance to hibernating colonies is a major threat to this species. Hibernating bats that are disturbed may lose much of their fat reserves, which are necessary for survival in winter when no insects are available.

NON-NATIVE MAMMALS . . . .

Several of the mammals described in this book are not native to the Great Smoky Mountains. The most infamous of these nonnatives is the wild hog. In most of the U.S. these animals are usually referred to as feral hogs, indicating that they are domestic livestock that have escaped and survived in the wild. In Great Smoky Mountains National Park, however, the origin was traced back to animals that escaped from a private hunting preserve near Hoopers Bald in western North Carolina in the early 1900s and spread to other areas, including the national park. Those animals were allegedly European in origin so the wild hog in the national park is often referred to as the European wild boar. In reality, wild hogs in the national park are a hybrid of European wild boar and feral or domestic hogs. Although they possess most of the physical characteristics of wild boar, an increasing number of animals have characteristics of feral or domestic hogs, including brown or spotted coloration, or white hair on the face and legs. Because the wild boar causes extensive damage to native animals and plants, the National Park Service has an active shooting and trapping program to control the population.

In the red fox chapter you will learn that there is still an ongoing debate whether this species is truly native. Because its introduction into North America likely occurred a long time ago, most mammalogists would consider this a native species. Much more recently (1980s), the coyote established itself prominently in the Great Smoky Mountains. Although its range expansion was facilitated by people, it is a highly adaptable animal and may eventually have reached the eastern U.S. by itself, especially now that the gray wolf and red wolf do not live here anymore.

Finally, there are three members of the Muridae family (old world rats and mice) that are not native. The most ubiquitous of those is the house mouse, which now occurs throughout the world and has the largest distribution of any mammal on earth. Two other species are the black rat and the Norway rat.

EXTIRPATED AND REINTRODUCED SPECIES . . . . . .

Large mammals often are most vulnerable to overhunting and

habitat changes so several became extirpated well before the establishment of Great Smoky Mountains National Park. American bison occurred in low densities but were extirpated in this area sometime around the late 18th century. Similarly, elk became extirpated in North Carolina by the late 1700s and in Tennessee by the mid 1800s. From the first European settlements until establishment of the national park, carnivores were relentlessly pursued. The last gray wolf was killed in the 1890s and the last eastern cougar was killed in 1920. Less clear is the record on the fisher, a medium-sized member of the weasel family. It is considered extinct in the national park area. However, although records exist for this species in the southern Appalachian region, it is uncertain whether this species ever occurred in the area that is now encompassed by the national park. The disappearance of river otters was related to trapping and hunting, but sedimentation and pollution of mountain streams from logging operations also contributed to its demise.

A primary mission of the National Park Service is to preserve native plants and animals on the lands it manages. If deemed feasible, the National Park Service may choose to reintroduce species that have been extirpated. During the last two decades, several attempts to reintroduce a number of mammals have occurred. The task of returning species to the wild is very complicated, particularly for mammals, and requires careful planning and monitoring. Returning a species like the American bison, for example, is currently not seriously considered because the socio-economic challenges are substantial and habitat areas within the national park are limited. An experimental reintroduction of red wolves during the 1990s was terminated because many wolves did not establish home ranges within the national park and wolf pups experienced high mortality. Depending on the species, however, reintroductions can be successful. The most successful reintroduction was that of the river otter during the 1980s and early 1990s. The river otter is now well established in the national park area. A reintroduction of elk is ongoing and time will tell whether it will be successful. The national park has also served as the population source for reintroductions elsewhere. For example, a small population of black bears currently persists in the Big South Fork National River and Recreation Area on the border of Kentucky and Tennessee. The founders of that population came from Great Smoky Mountains National Park.

WILDLIFE'S FUTURE . . . .

The future of wildlife in Great Smoky Mountains National Park is reasonably secure for most mammals. The national park is well protected and most mammals have healthy population levels. The national park is also connected with national forest and state lands, particularly along the North Carolina boundary. Habitat will remain protected on those lands as well, allowing important exchange among wildlife populations to maintain healthy demographics and genetic diversity. However, with the increasing popularity of the Great Smoky Mountains for tourism, outdoor recreation, or a place to live, the pressures and demands on the resources of this area will increase. Of all the mammals in the national park, wide-ranging species would be affected most by habitat loss and fragmentation. Black bears, for example, need large areas of relatively undisturbed forest. With increasing development in areas near the national park, young dispersing bears may have few places to go in the future, resulting in more human encounters and nuisance incidences, which, in turn, may lead to high bear mortality. In years when foods are limited, even bears that normally stay well inside the national park will leave the park in search of food, increasing the risk of mortality. As the experimental red wolf reintroduction demonstrated, developed areas near the national park limit the prospects of reintroducing large carnivores. Similarly, the future of the elk reintroduction project will depend in large part on whether damage to croplands near the national park boundaries can be limited.

With growing tourism and development near the national park, wildlife managers will increasingly have to resolve human-wildlife conflicts. Whereas coyotes were a novelty in Cades Cove just a decade ago, some individuals have now become habituated to humans, waiting for food hand-outs from passing cars. Similarly, the black bear's keen sense of smell easily entices it to human foods left on a picnic table, garbage, or hand-outs. Despite proactive management by federal, state, and city managers, nuisance black bears remain a problem in areas like Gatlinburg. Once bears become habituated to humans, they lose their instinctive fear of people and may become unpredictable and dangerous, damaging property and injuring humans. Studies have shown that the life span of habituated bears is shortened substantially as they become more vulnerable to poaching or vehicle collisions. This is a good example of why it is important not to feed any wildlife or to allow access to garbage and other types of human-related foods.

In the end, the future of wildlife in Great Smoky Mountains National Park and surrounding areas may be determined more by unpredictable but potentially significant events. No one was able to document the impact of the disappearance of the American chestnut on wildlife in the early 1900s, but many mammalian species likely were adversely affected by the loss of this major food source. At the beginning of the 21st century, many wildlife species once again face events that may substantially alter the forests of the Great Smoky Mountains due to numerous forest pests, including the gypsy moth, sudden oak death, and the hemlock woolly adelgid. Mammals are adaptable and can adjust their behavior to respond to gradual changes in their environment, but our stewardship will be crucial to protect these mountain ecosystems from the tremendous natural and people-related pressures that threaten wildlife's long-term survival.

—*F. van Manen, Research Ecologist, U.S. Geological Survey*

Using This Guide

Red Wolf

The red wolf is an endangered species endemic to the southeastern U.S. It is intermediate in size compared with the larger gray wolf and the smaller coyote. It is very similar in appearance to the coyote, but its fur is more tawny-cinnamon colored, mixed with gray and black, and is darkest on the back. The tail has a black tip. A black color phase has been observed in the past. Like other members of the *Canidae* (dog family), red wolves walk on their toes (digitigrade).

◆ **STATUS & HABITAT**—Red wolves prefer forest margins, which provide access to vegetative cover and open fields where they hunt

181

SCIENTIFIC NAME

STATUS

Species was:

- **Reintroduced**—Originally native but was eliminated by human actions, and brought back to the area.
by the National Park Service in the last 30 years.
- **Extirpated**—Currently extinct in the park.
- **Non-native**—A foreign species brought to the area by humans.
- **Endangered**—Federally listed as in danger of extinction.

LENGTH

Including tail

WEIGHT

ELEVATION

Gold shading indicates at what elevations the species is typically found in the Great Smoky Mountains.

Map of Great Smoky Mountains National Park

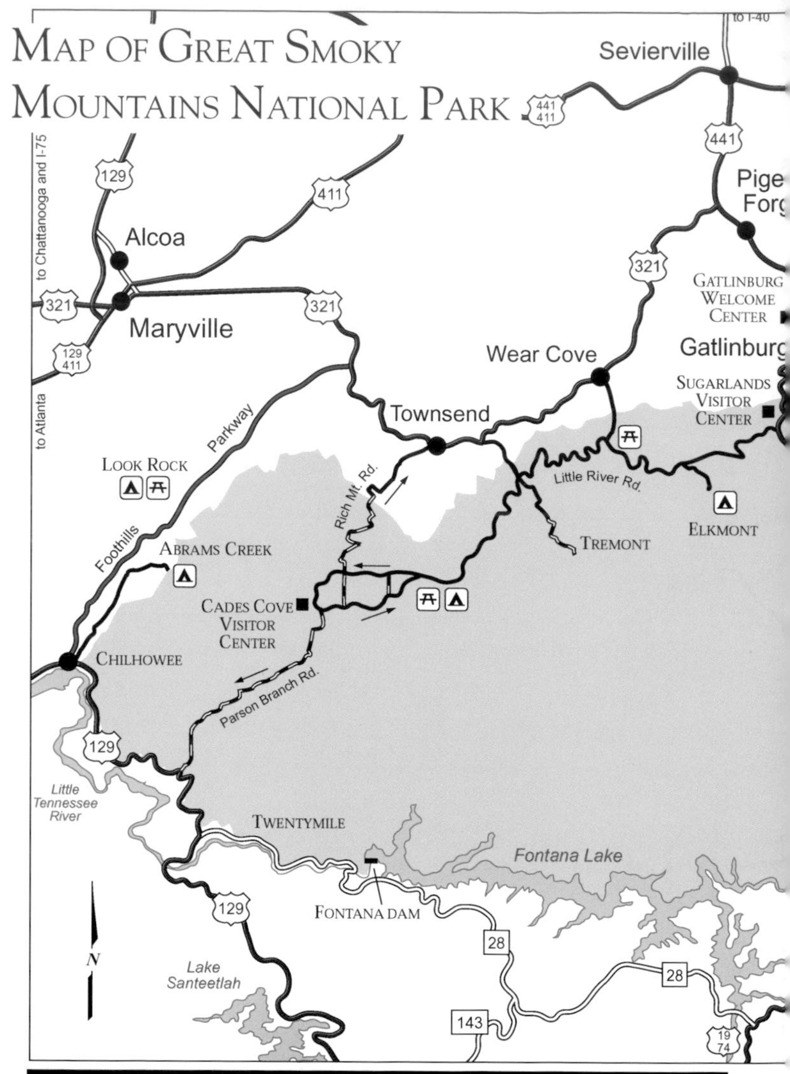

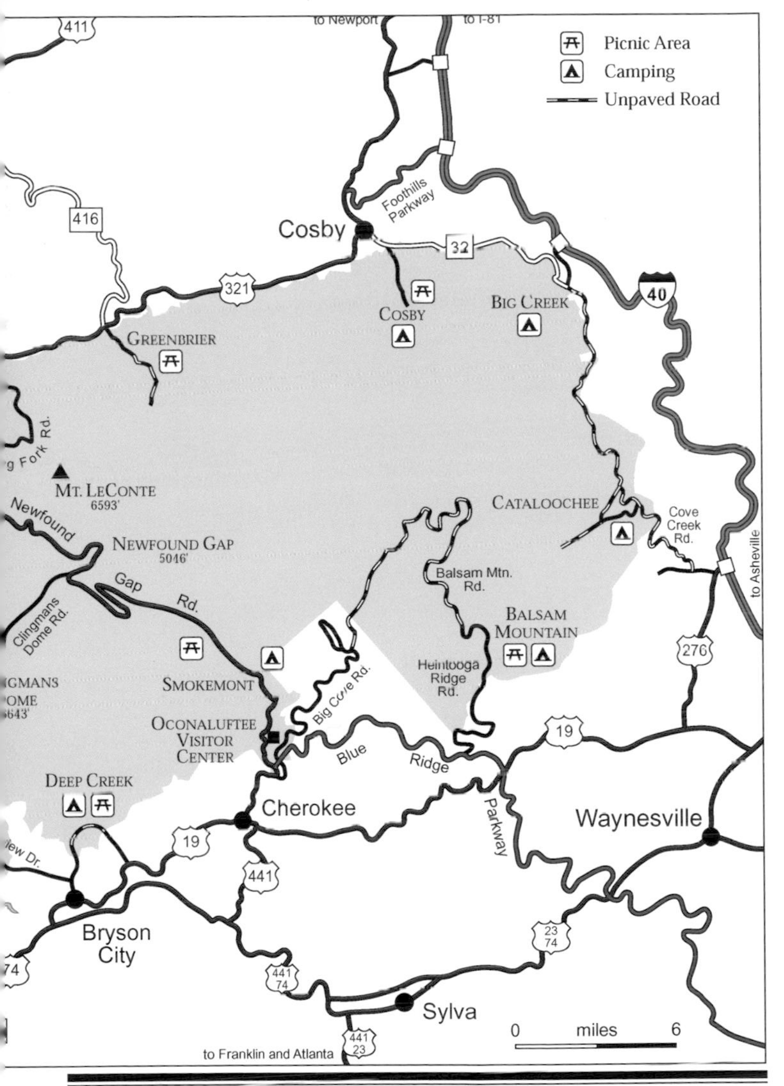
411
to Newport
to I-81
Picnic Area
Camping
Unpaved Road
416
Foothills Parkway
Cosby
32
321
40
Cosby
Big Creek
Greenbrier
Mt. LeConte
6593'
Newfound
Newfound Gap
5046'
Gap
Rd.
Clingmans Dome Rd.
Cataloochee
Cove Creek Rd.
to Asheville
Balsam Mtn. Rd.
Balsam Mountain
276
Heintooga Ridge Rd.
Big Cove Rd.
Smokemont
Oconaluftee Visitor Center
Blue
Ridge
Parkway
19
Deep Creek
Cherokee
Waynesville
19
441
Bryson City
74
23
74
441
74
Sylva
0
miles
6
441
23
to Franklin and Atlanta

Opossums

ORDER DIDELPHIMORHIA

(Marsupialia)

Family Didelphidae

Virginia Opossum

Ann and Rob Simpson

VIRGINIA OPOSSUM

Maslowski Wildlife Productions

Didelphis virginiana

22" - 36" length
(55 - 90 cm)

2.2 - 10 lbs
(1 - 4.5 kg)

No other mammal in the national park can be confused with the Virginia opossum. It is the only marsupial north of Mexico. It has a pointed snout with white cheeks and a black eye stripe. Its fur color is gray but can vary from pale to almost black The nearly naked tail is scaly and is almost as long as the body.

The opossum has several unique features, including an abdominal pouch in which newborns are carried after birth and where they nurse. Most young are born from late winter through early summer after a very short gestation period of 13 days. The newborns are miniscule (0.6"; 14 mm), weigh less than 0.035 ounce

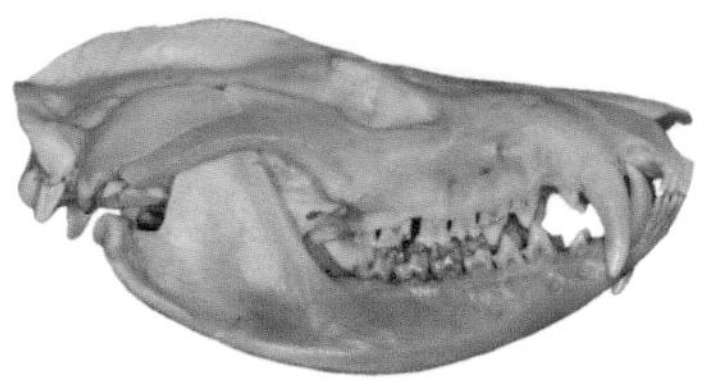
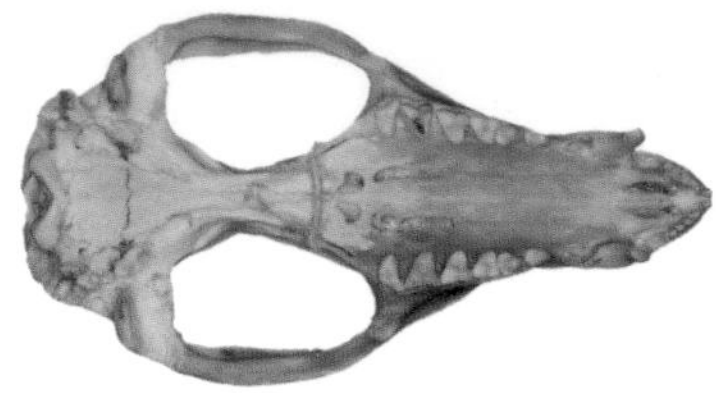

(1 gram), and are helpless. Young are weaned after about 100 days. Some females have up to two litters per year, with as many as 15 newborns per litter.

One of their well-known behaviors is "playing possum" and involves a body state in which they feign death. This behavior can be effective when faced with a severe threat of predation. In one instance, an opossum that was released after being captured as part of a research project in Cades Cove walked into a creek, stayed on the bottom for about two minutes, and then came out and walked away.

◆ **STATUS & HABITAT**—Opossums can be found throughout the national park, except for the highest elevations. They use many different habitat types, but seem to prefer deciduous woodlands along streams. They can also be found near picnic areas and campgrounds, where they search for human foods. Opossums are highly omnivorous. They forage along erratic routes, often changing direction while investigating potential food sources with their paws and snouts. Home ranges are typically 50 acres or less.

The typical life span of opossums is only about two years, but many individuals will not live that long because of collisions with vehicles and predation. Opossums are nocturnal but are occasionally seen during the day in winter. Although they seem sluggish, they are adept climbers, using their prehensile tail and opposable toe on the hindfoot to grasp branches. They are strong swimmers and can stay underwater for extended periods of time.

Opossums can be found east of the Rocky Mountains from southern Canada to northern Mexico. They have gradually moved north over the last centuries, taking advantage of human food resources with expanding human settlements. The northern boundary of the range is limited by climate and lack of food during winter. Opossums also now occur along the west coast of the U.S. because of transplantations by humans.

Steve Greer/SteveGreerPhotography.com

Opossums have prehensile tails which can grasp branches.

opossum tracks

Look for:
- *Five toes on hind foot, with three clustered middle toes*
- *"Big toe" does not have a claw*
- *Front tracks measure 1 - 2 5/16" long*

opossum scat

Shrews

ORDER INSECTIVORA

Family Soricidae

Masked Shrew
Southeastern Shrew
Water Shrew
Smoky Shrew
Long-tailed Shrew
Pygmy Shrew
Northern Short-tailed Shrew
Least Shrew

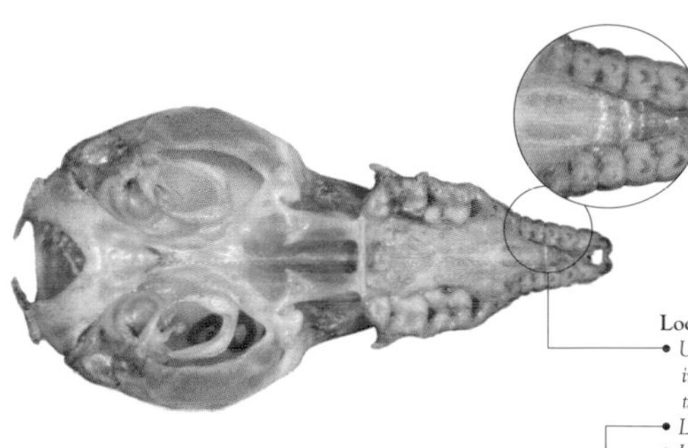

Look for:

- *Unicuspid teeth—modified incisor, canine, and premolar teeth*
- *Long, narrow snout (rostrum)*
- *Upper incisors are large and hooked, like a falcon beak*
- *Tips of all teeth are often dark chestnut in color due to iron (North American shrews also known as red-toothed shrews)*

shrew tracks

Front tracks measure 3/16" - 3/8" long, depending on species

shrew scat

size, tail length comparison of six common shrews

(l-r: smoky, masked, southeastern, pygmy, northern short-tailed, and least shrews)

MASKED SHREW

Phil Myers, Museum of Zoology, University of Michigan

Sorex cinereus

2 4/5" - 4 9/10" length
(7.1 - 12.5 cm)

1/10 - 3/10 oz
(2.2 - 7.8 g)

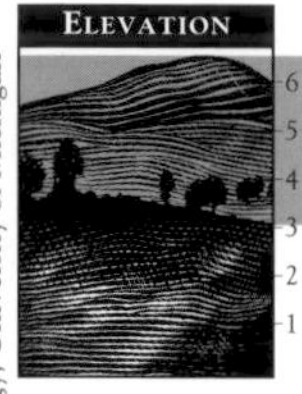

The origin of the name masked shrew is unknown since this shrew has no mask. Its sides and back are grayish to dark brown with a pale grayish brown underside. The tail is relatively long, covered with short hairs, and is indistinctly bicolored. The fur is very short and velvety to allow for minimal resistance as the animal moves through its burrows. This species possesses a relatively long rostrum (snout), which, along with its pincer-like incisors, allows it to probe very narrow spaces for food. The eyes are minute and the ears are hidden in the fur. It possesses musk glands on its flanks that produce a strong musky odor that may deter predators.

◆ **STATUS & HABITAT**— In the southern Appalachians these shrews prefer moist deciduous and mixed forests that have deep leaf litter. They are also found in moist meadows and sphagnum bogs. The presence of moss-covered rocks, decaying logs, and exposed roots and stumps creates an even more suitable habitat.

The masked shrew is very common in the southern Appalachian Mountains and is one of the smallest species of mammals in the South. It is not commonly observed or identified since it spends most of its time rapidly foraging around in leaf litter. In the Americas this shrew occurs from the Atlantic coast of Canada to Alaska. Its range extends south to Washington, down the Rocky Mountains to Arizona and from Maine through the Appalachian Mountains to northwestern South Carolina. It is one of the most widespread mammals in North America.

Masked shrews are eaten by foxes, weasels, bobcats, snakes, and birds of prey. Very little research has been done on this species in

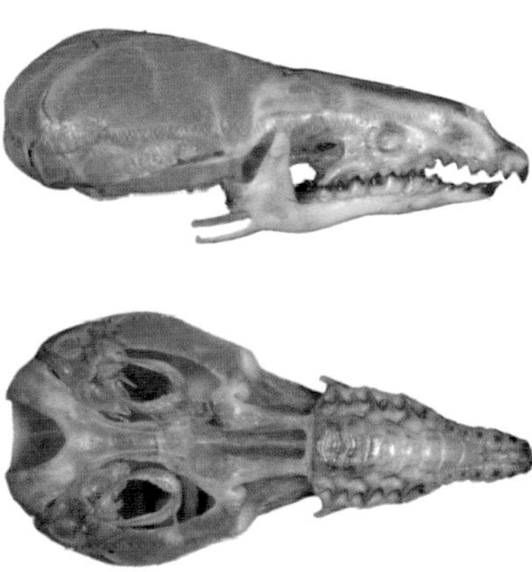

the South, but northern population densities have varied from five to close to 100 per acre. Their life span in the wild is no longer than one to two years.

Masked shrews eat snails, slugs, insects, ants, spiders, and worms. They will feast on dead vertebrates and occasionally on plant materials. As is the rule for all shrews, this species has a high metabolic rate and consumes its body weight in food each day.

These shrews use the burrow systems of small rodents and also construct their own subsurface burrows to seek out prey. When seen, they are usually darting about on the surface and under the leaf litter, constantly probing with their noses and making high pitched whistles that are probably used in echolocation. Young display an interesting movement behavior called caravanning. Individuals assemble in single file with the nose of one in the rump of another as they move about.

James F. Parnell

Edward Pivorun

Sorex longirostris
2 7/10" - 4 1/2 " length
(6.8 - 11.6 cm)

1/10 - 1/5 oz
(2.0 - 5.8 g)

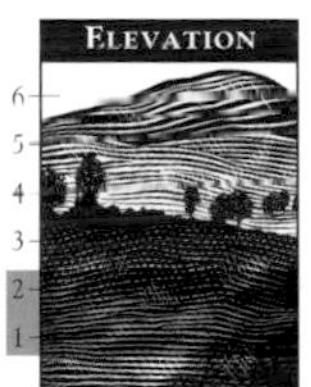

The southeastern shrew's sides and back are reddish brown and the underside is gray. The tail is long and sparsely covered with short hairs. This species is one of the long-tailed shrews and only the long-tailed pygmy shrew is smaller. The fur is very short and velvety to allow for minimal resistance as the animal moves through its burrows. It possesses a relatively long rostrum (snout), which along with its pincer-like incisors, allows it to probe spaces for food. The eyes are minute, but the ears are partially exposed above the fur.

◆ **STATUS & HABITAT**—The Southeastern shrew is very common in parts of the Southeast; however, this species is not common at higher elevations and only three specimens have been documented in the park. The distribution of the masked shrew and the Southeastern shrew generally do not overlap. This mammal is not commonly observed or identified since it spends most of its time rapidly foraging around in leaf litter and grassy areas. In the Americas this shrew occurs from Maryland to Indiana and south to Florida and Louisiana.

These shrews prefer moist habitats such as swamps, marshes, and stream and river bottomlands. Many individuals have been observed in disturbed habitats such as abandoned fields and thickets of brush and saplings with a thick cover of grass, sedges, blackberry, and honeysuckle. In the mountains this shrew has been observed primarily in grassy fields and the borders of forested areas.

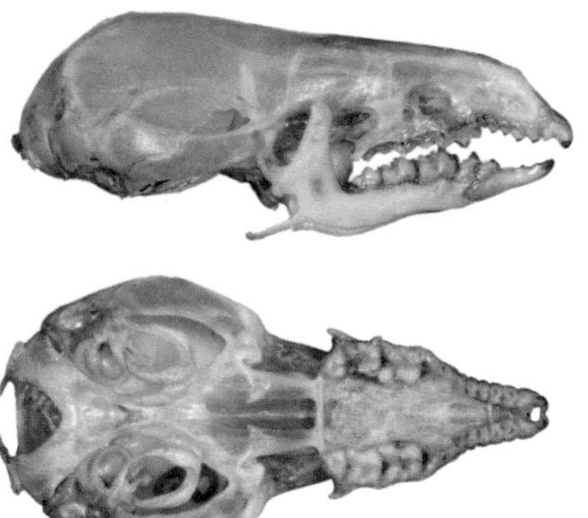

This species is preyed upon by foxes, opossums, snakes, owls and other birds of prey. Very little research has been done on it. One study found population densities of 12 to 18 shrews per acre. Usually one to six young are born per litter and two to three litters are produced per year. Their life span in the wild is probably no longer than one to one and a half years.

Southeastern shrews eat insects, spiders, slugs, snails, and centipedes.

These shrews display both nocturnal and diurnal activity. They utilize the burrow systems of small rodents, other shrews, and moles. Nests of dried leaves and grass are constructed just below or in rotten logs.

Sorex palustris

5 3/10" - 6 7/10" length
(13.5 - 17.0 cm)

3/10 - 3/5 oz
(8.0 - 18.8 g)

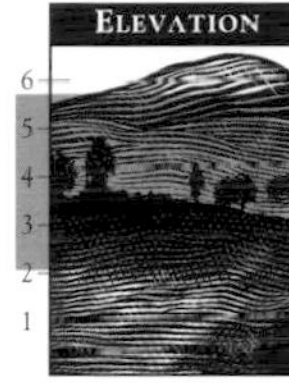

© Dwight Kuhn

The water shrew's sides and back are dark brown to black and the underside is a paler grayish white. The tail is distinctly bicolored. This species is the largest *Sorex* in the East and possesses the longest tail of any of the eastern *Sorex* species. The fur is very short and velvety. This adaptation traps air which waterproofs the fur and adds buoyancy to the body. A fringe of stiff hairs is found on the sides of each foot and on each toe. The toes on the rear feet possess partial webbing. The eyes are minute and the ears are mostly hidden in the fur.

◆ **STATUS & HABITAT**—The water shrew is not a very common shrew in the Southeast; in fact it was not until 1950 that one of these shrews was found in the park. They are primarily found near streams at higher elevations in the Southeast. The forests associated with these habitats are coniferous or mixed forests with an abundance of logs, rocks, crevices and exposed roots. This mammal is not commonly observed since it spends most of its time rapidly foraging around and in mountain streams. In the Americas this shrew occurs from the Atlantic coast of Canada to southeastern Alaska. Its range extends south in the western United States down the Rocky Mountains to Utah and New Mexico and down the Sierra Nevada to California. In the East and Midwest this species is found from Maine to Pennsylvania and in Minnesota and Michigan. In the Southeast it is found only in the Appalachian Mountains from West Virginia to north Georgia.

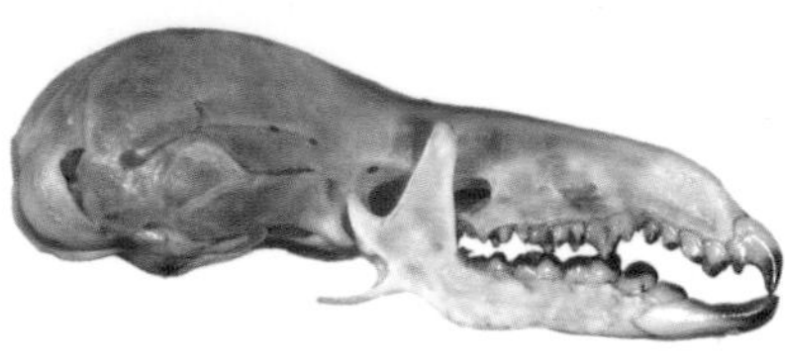

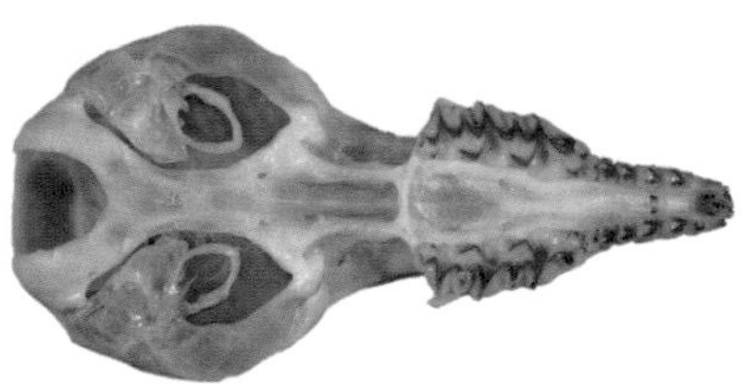

Many animals prey upon water shrews, including trout, bass, snakes, weasels, mink, owls, and other birds of prey. In turn, water shrews eat insect larvae, snails, slugs, flatworms, fish, frogs, fish eggs, aquatic invertebrates, and tadpoles.

Very little research has been done on this species in the Southeast. Studies have found population densities are relatively low compared to other shrew species. Usually four to ten young are born per litter and two to three litters are produced per year. Life span in the wild is probably no longer than one and a half years.

These shrews display both nocturnal and diurnal activity and actively seek prey in the winter, even under the ice. They are excellent swimmers and can dive to the bottom of streambeds for 15 - 40 second intervals. They are very buoyant and "pop" to the surface. The hairs on their feet trap bubbles of air, allowing them to "walk" on water, thus their nickname "water walkers."

© Dwight Kuhn

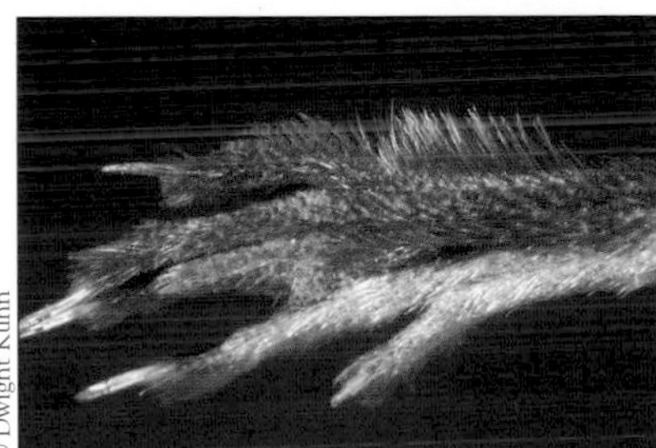

© Dwight Kuhn

Smoky Shrew

Edward Pivorun

Sorex fumeus

4″ - 5″ length
(10.0 - 12.7 cm)

1/5 - 2/5 oz
(5.5 - 11.0 g)

The smoky shrew's sides and back are grayish to dark brown and the underside is gray. In winter the dorsal fur is grayer in color. In general, the browner color of the masked shrew aids in separating these two species. The smoky shrew's tail is long, covered with short hairs, and is bicolored. In adults the tip of the tail may lose all its hairs and become rounded and smooth. The fur is very short and velvety to allow for minimal resistance as the animal moves through its burrows. This species possesses a relatively short rostrum (snout). The eyes are minute and the ears are partially exposed above the fur.

◆ **STATUS & HABITAT**—The smoky shrew is very common in the higher elevations of the southern Appalachian Mountains and is one of the larger species of long-tailed shrew in the South. This mammal is not commonly observed or identified since it spends most of its time rapidly foraging around in leaf litter. In the Americas this shrew occurs from the Atlantic coast of southeastern Canada to Lake Superior. Its range extends south from New England to Indiana and through the Appalachian Mountains to northwestern South Carolina. In the southern Appalachians these shrews prefer moist deciduous, mixed, and spruce-fir forests that have deep leaf litter. The presence of moss-covered rocks, deep crevices in rocky slopes, streams, decaying logs, and exposed roots and stumps creates an even more suitable habitat.

This species is prey for foxes, weasels, bobcats, raccoon, and birds of prey. Very little research has been done on it in the South, but northern population densities have varied from five to close to 50 per acre. Usually two to eight young are born per litter and two to three litters are produced per year. Life span in the wild is no longer than one and a half years. In fact, studies have shown that almost the entire population of adult shrews dies out after the fall breeding season. This species, along with the other shrews, consumes many insect forest pests.

Smoky shrews eat insects, sowbugs, snails, spiders, centipedes, worms, salamanders, mice, and birds. As is the rule for all shrews, this species has a high metabolic rate and consumes about half of its body weight in food each day.

These shrews display both nocturnal and diurnal activity. They use the burrow systems of small rodents, other shrews, and moles. When seen, these shrews are darting about on the surface and under the leaf litter, constantly probing with their noses and making high-pitched noises that are probably used in echolocation.

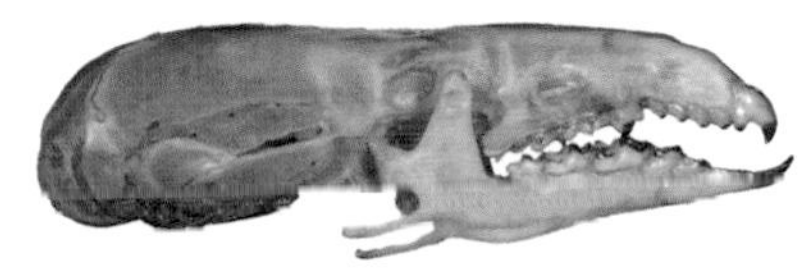

LONG-TAILED SHREW

Edward Pivorun

Sorex dispar

4″ - 5 2/5″ length
(10.3 - 13.7 cm)

1/10 - 3/10 oz
(3.1 - 8.9 g)

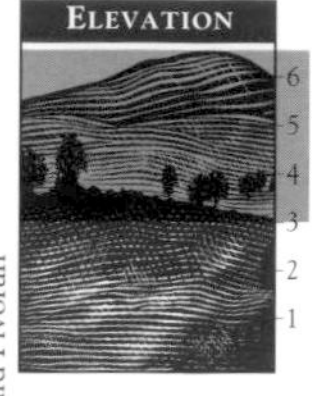

The long-tailed shrew's sides and back are slate gray with a comparably colored underside. The tail is very long (generally longer than any other *Sorex* species), thick, covered with short hairs, and is indistinctly bicolored. The fur is very short and velvety to allow for minimal resistance as the animal moves through its burrows. This species possesses a relatively long and narrow rostrum (snout), which, along with its pincer-like incisors, allows it to probe very narrow spaces for food. The body is also relatively slim for a *Sorex* species. The eyes are minute and the ears are hidden in the fur.

◆ **STATUS & HABITAT**—The long-tailed shrew is also known as the rock shrew and has a very restricted preferred habitat. It is one of the most difficult mammals to study and little is known about its natural history. In the Americas this shrew occurs from New Brunswick south through the mountains to North Carolina and Tennessee.

This shrew is probably prey for foxes, snakes, and birds of prey. Very little research has been done on this species in the South. Usually two to five young are born per litter. Life span in the wild is probably no longer than one year.

Throughout their range these shrews prefer moist and cool higher altitude coniferous and mixed forests with an abundance of moss covered logs and rocks and proximity to mountain streams. In parts of their range the preferred habitat consists of natural talus slopes, boulder fields, and man-made talus slopes on the sides of roads.

Long-tailed shrews eat insects, spiders, ants, and centipedes.

They are active mornings, evenings, and at night. They seem to spend most of their time in the passages between rocks and boulders and along the rocky borders of mountain streams. The long tail is considered a counterbalance structure that aids them in climbing over and among the rocks that make up their habitat.

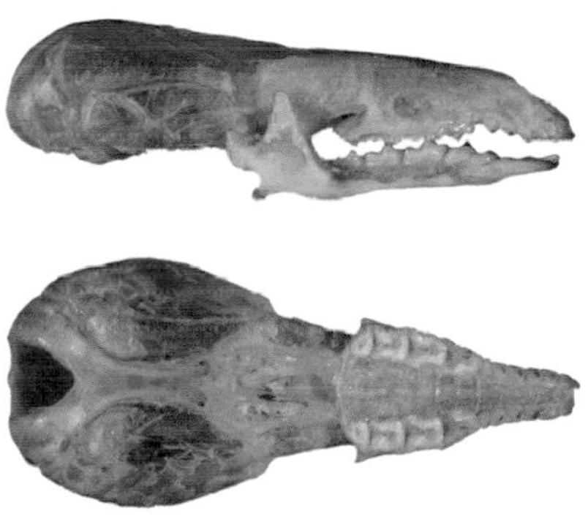

Pygmy Shrew

Edward Pivorun

Sorex (Microsorex) hoyi

2 2/5" - 4 1/5" length (6.2 - 10.6 cm)

1/20 - 1/10 oz (2.0 - 4.0 g)

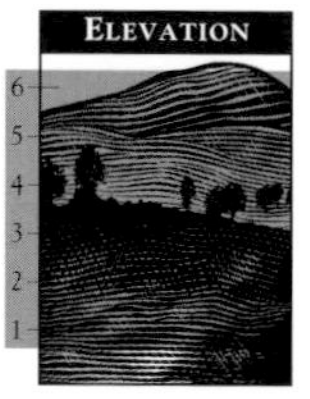

The pygmy shrew's sides and back are dark reddish to gray brown with a paler grayish underside. The tail is relatively long, covered with short hairs, and is indistinctly bicolored. The fur is very short and velvety to allow for minimal resistance as the animal moves through its burrows. This species possesses a relatively long rostrum (snout), which, along with its pincer-like incisors, allows it to probe very narrow spaces for food. This species of *Sorex* possesses minute 3rd and 5th unicuspids and only three unicuspids are visible from the side. All other eastern *Sorex* species only possess a minute 5th unicuspid and four unicuspids are visible from the side. The eyes are minute and the ears are hidden in the fur.

◆ **STATUS & HABITAT**—The pygmy shrew is the smallest shrew in the New World and is one of the rarest or most difficult mammals to find in its southeastern range. In the Americas this shrew occurs south of the tundra from the Atlantic coast of Canada to Alaska. Its range extends south to Washington, Montana, the Dakotas, Minnesota, Wisconsin and from Maine through the Appalachian Mountains to north Georgia.

This species is the rarest shrew in the park. It is preyed upon by foxes, snakes, and birds of prey. Very little research has been done on this species in the South. Usually two to eight young are born per litter and normally one to two litters are produced per year. Their life span in the wild is probably no longer than one year.

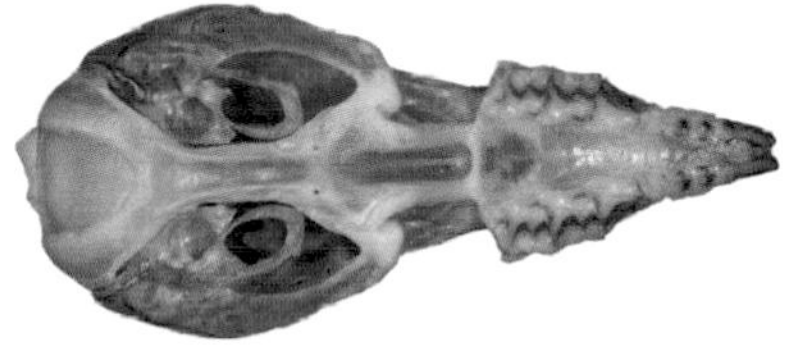

In the southern Appalachians these shrews prefer moist deciduous and mixed forests that have deep leaf litter and rotting logs. They can also be found on ridgetops, mountain slopes, and in grasslands and forest edges.

Pygmy shrews eat insects, spiders, ants, seeds, berries, and worms.

These shrews display nocturnal and diurnal activity. They climb vegetation and will stand on their hind legs kangaroo fashion. This species has well developed musk glands on its flanks that may be used for marking sites. Nests are constructed just below the surface under logs, roots, or in burrows.

Northern Short-tailed Shrew

Edward Pivorun

Blarina brevicauda

3″ - 5 1/2″ length
(7.5 - 13.9 cm)

2/5 - 1 1/10 oz
(11 - 30 g)

The northern short-tailed shrew's sides and back are dark slate in color, the underside is paler and the tops of the feet are pinkish gray. The tail is short, slender, and hairy. The fur is very short and velvety to allow for minimal resistance as the animal moves through its burrows. This species possesses a relatively short snout. The eyes are minute and the ears are hidden by the fur. This shrew is the heaviest of all eastern species of shrew and produces a strong musky odor that may deter predators.

◆ **STATUS & HABITAT**—The northern short-tailed shrew is very common in virtually every forested area with a thick layer of leaves and organic

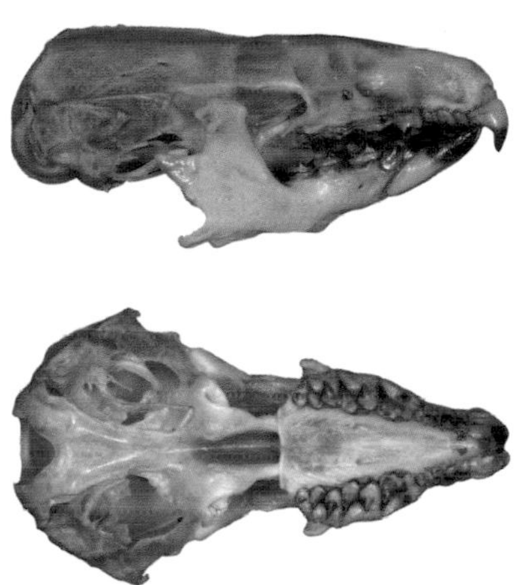

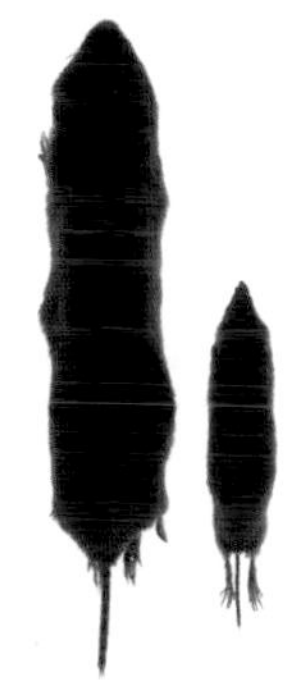

Tail length comparison of northern short-tailed (left) and least shrews

material. They prefer moist soils and are found near bogs, streams, and swamps. They are also found in grassy, weedy, and brushy fields with relatively loose soils.

This mammal is not commonly observed or identified since it spends most of its time hidden by leaf litter. In the Americas this shrew lives from the Atlantic coast of Canada across southern Canada to southwestern Saskatchewan and its range extends south to Nebraska, Kentucky, and Virginia through the Appalachian Mountains to Tennessee, North and South Carolina, Georgia and Alabama. In the southern states the range of the northern short-tailed shrew slightly overlaps the southern short-tailed shrew's range.

This species is prey for foxes, bobcats, weasels, snakes, owls and other birds of prey. Usually three to nine young are born per litter and two to three litters may be produced per year. Life span in the wild is no longer than one to two years. This species, along with the other shrews, consumes many insect pests.

Northern short-tailed shrews eat insects, millipedes, snails, slugs, worms, rodents, and other shrews. Plant roots, beechnuts, fungi (genus *Endogone*), and seeds are also consumed. This species is one of the few mammals that produces a toxin. The salivary glands of this species produce a toxin that is both a neurotoxin and hemotoxin and is chewed into its victim. This allows this shrew to subdue larger mammalian prey. It also paralyzes invertebrate prey and keeps this food item "fresh" for days after being subdued and stored. Bites to pets, such as domestic cats, are probably painful but not lethal. As is the rule for all shrews, this species has a high metabolic rate and consumes one half or more of its body weight in food each day.

When seen, these shrews are darting about on the surface and under leaf litter, constantly probing with their noses. Researchers have shown that this species uses echolocation to navigate around its environment.

Cryptotis parva

2 2/5" - 3 3/10" length
(6.1 - 9.2 cm)

1/10 - 2/5 oz
(2.8 - 10.0 g)

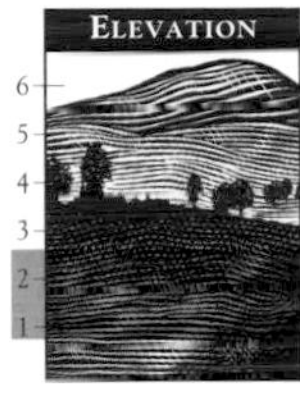

Edward P. voruz

The least shrew's sides and back are dark grayish brown and its underside is gray. In general the brownish color of this shrew can aid one in distinguishing this species from the slate gray short-tailed shrew. The tail is short, slender, and is indistinctly bicolored. The fur is very short and velvety to allow for minimal resistance as the animal moves through its burrows. This species possesses a relatively short rostrum (snout), which, along with its pincer like incisors, allows it to probe spaces for food. The eyes are minute and the ears are mostly hidden by the fur.

◆ **STATUS & HABITAT**—The least shrew is a relatively common shrew in the meadows, grasslands, and weedy sites of the eastern United States and is one of the short-tailed shrews. This mammal is not commonly observed since it spends most of its time hidden by grass. In the Americas this shrew occurs from the Atlantic coast of New York to South Dakota and its range extends south to Texas and

Florida and deep into Central America.

The least shrew is prey for skunks, bobcats, weasels, snakes, and owls. Very little research has been done on this species in the South, but northern population densities are two individuals per acre. Usually two to seven young are born per litter and four to five litters may be produced per year. Breeding has been observed in shrews that are one and a half to three months old. Life span in the wild is no longer than one to one and a half years. This species, along with the other shrew species, consumes many insect pests.

Least shrews eat insects, snails, spiders, slugs, worms, and an occasional frog or lizard. Generally only the internal organs of large insects are consumed. As is the rule for all shrews, this species has a high metabolism and consumes almost its body weight in food each day. Food hoarding has been reported for this species.

These shrews display both nocturnal and diurnal activity. Unlike most shrews, this species seems to be very social and gregarious. Records have documented more than 20 individuals sharing the same nest. They utilize the burrow systems of small rodents, other shrews, and moles. When seen, these shrews are darting about on the surface and in the grass, constantly probing with their noses and making high pitched squeaks and clicks. Their nests (two to five inch diameters) of dried leaves and grass are constructed just below the surface, under logs, roots, or rocks.

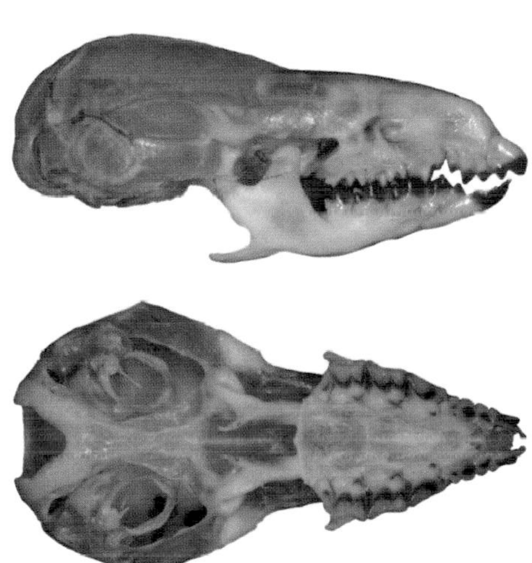

MOLES

ORDER INSECTIVORA

Family Talpidae

Hairy-tailed Mole
Eastern Mole
Star-nosed Mole

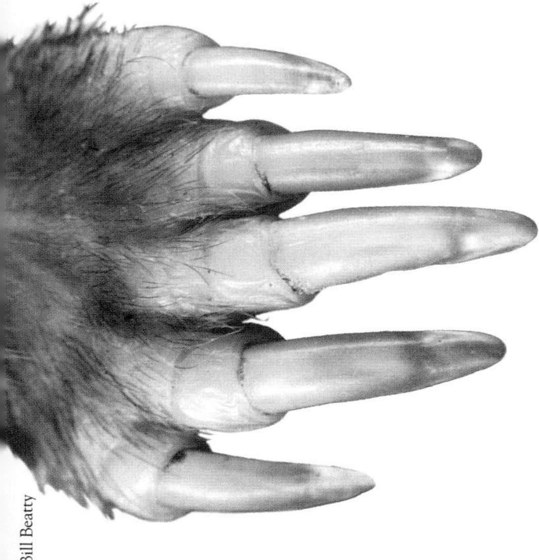

Bill Beatty

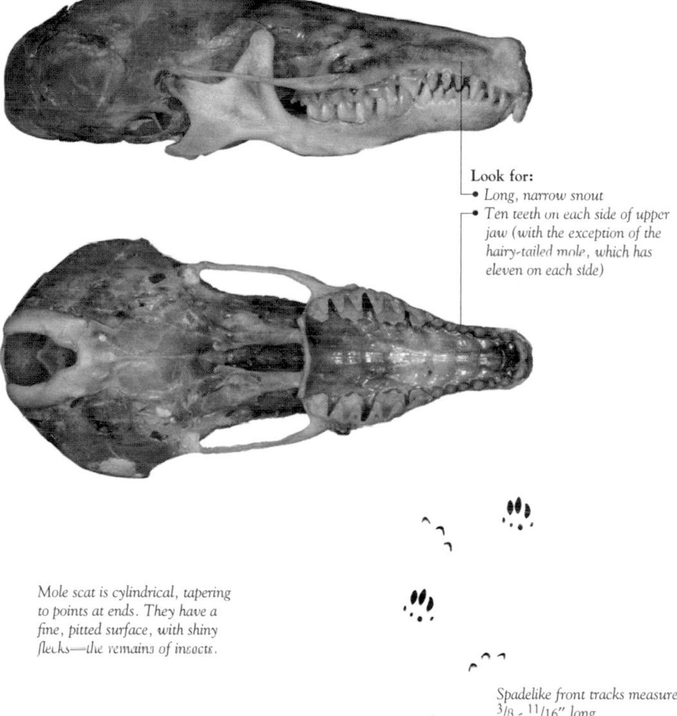

Mole scat is cylindrical, tapering to points at ends. They have a fine, pitted surface, with shiny flecks—the remains of insects.

Spadelike front tracks measure 3/8 - 11/16" long

mole tracks

HAIRY-TAILED MOLE

© Dwight Kuhn

Parascalops breweri

5 3/10" - 7" length
(13.5 - 17.6 cm)

1 2/5 - 2 3/10 oz
(40.0 - 65.0 g)

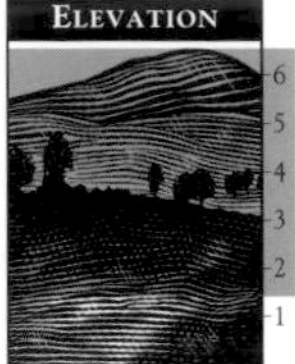

The hairy-tailed mole is generally the smallest mole in the East. The sides and back are black to dark slate with a paler underside. Unlike the other two species of eastern moles, this species has a short, hairy tail that is black and at times possesses a white tuft of hair at the tip. The fur is short and velvety to allow for minimal resistance as the animal moves through its burrows. A shared characteristic with other species of moles is the broad forefoot that possesses strong claws. The eyes are minute and the ears are hidden in the fur. The skull has a flat profile and the body is tapered at both ends.

◆ **STATUS & HABITAT**—The hairy-tailed mole is a relatively common mole in the mountainous regions of the eastern United

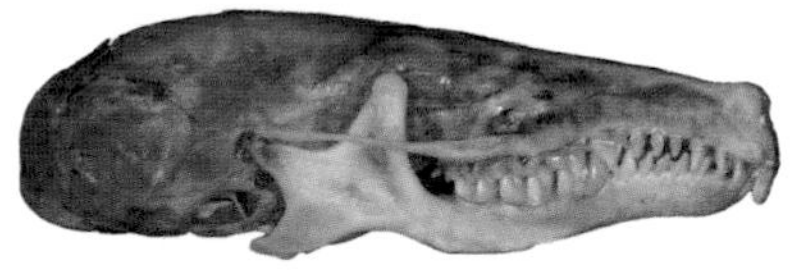

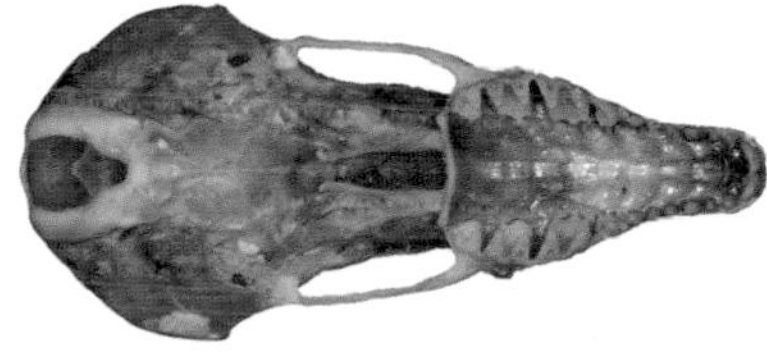

States. It is not commonly observed since it spends most of its time underground. In the Americas this mole occurs from southern Ontario and Quebec south to Ohio. It lives in most of New England and it follows the Appalachian Mountains south to South Carolina and Tennessee.

This species is prey for foxes, opossum, snakes, and birds of prey. As many as 10 or more moles can be found per acre in exceptional habitat. They help to till and aerate the soil. Usually four to five young are born per litter and these young can in turn breed when they are 10 months old. Usually one litter is produced per year. Generally these moles live four to five years in the wild.

Hairy-tailed moles prefer mountain deciduous and conifer forests with a light, well drained soil. This species avoids soils that are wet or predominantly clay. They are found mainly in forests with a thick groundcover and generally do not overlap with the eastern mole in the Appalachian Mountains.

Favorite mole meals consist of beetles, earthworms, ants, centipedes, millipedes, and other arthropods.

These moles display both nocturnal and diurnal activity. They form both subsurface and deep tunnel systems (10″-20″ below the surface) with the deeper systems used in winter. This species forages extensively on the surface during the night. Nests of dried leaves and grass are constructed in the deeper burrows.

Eastern Mole

Bob Gress

Scalopus aquaticus

4″ - 8 1/5″ length
(10.3 - 20.8 cm)

1 1/10 - 5 oz
(32.0 - 140.0 g)

The sides and back of the eastern mole are brownish black to silvery gray with a paler grayish underside. Yellow to orange stains are visible because of secretions from glands located on the head and underside. The tail is short and sparsely covered with hair and functions as an organ for touch. The fur is short and velvety to allow for minimal resistance as the animal moves through its burrows. A shared characteristic with other species of moles is the broad forefoot that possesses strong claws. The toes are partially webbed. The eyes are minute and covered with skin and the ears are hidden in the fur. The snout is very flexible, naked and the nasal openings face upward. Both the nasal area and the feet have a pink to white coloration. These moles have a strong musky odor that deters predators.

◆ **STATUS & HABITAT**—The eastern mole is a relatively common mole in the South, though it is not often observed since it spends most of its time underground. It prefers well-drained soils in meadows, open forests, or fields, especially where there are loamy or sandy soils. It eats earthworms, larval and adult insects, snails, slugs, centipedes, and ants. Eastern moles will also consume seeds and plant parts.

This species is prey for skunks, foxes, coyotes, snakes, and birds of prey. Its burrowing tills and aerates the soil. Usually two to five young are born per litter and one litter is produced per year. These moles normally live from four to six years in the wild.

In the Americas this mole occurs from Massachusetts west to North Dakota and south to Florida, eastern Texas and parts of northern Mexico.

Eastern moles display both nocturnal and diurnal activity. They form both temporary subsurface and permanent deep tunnels. The subsurface tunnels serve as feeding burrows and can extend to distances of over 1,000 feet. Researchers have clocked these moles creating burrow systems at a rate of 18 feet per hour. The subsurface tunnels are delineated by ridges of soil at the surface. These moles do not actually make many "molehills." The deeper tunnels are six inches to three feet below the surface and contain the nest chamber. Eastern moles are solitary except during the breeding season.

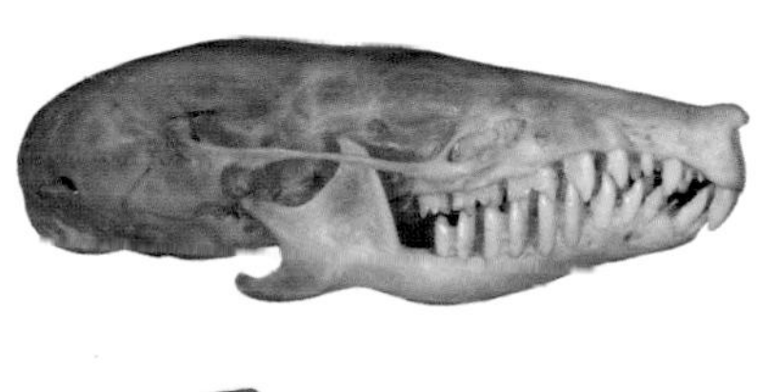

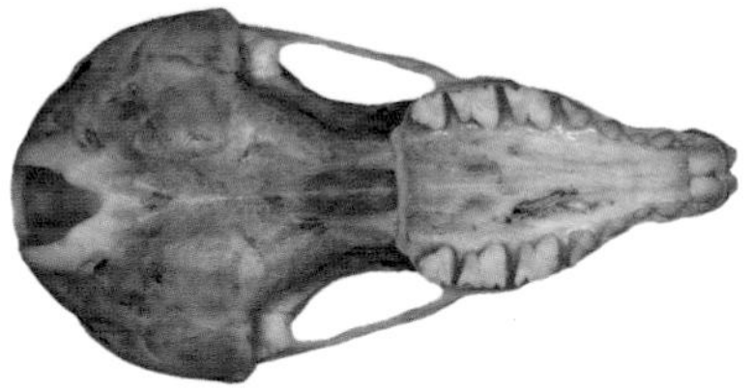

Star-nosed Mole

© Dwight Kuhn

Condylura cristata

5 1/5" - 9" length
(13.2 - 23.0 cm)

1 1/10 - 3 oz
(30.0 - 85.0 g)

The star-nosed mole is named for the 22 fleshy, finger-like projections surrounding its nostrils. These projections contain thousands of sensory structures called Eimer's organs. These sensors aid the animal in "feeling" its environment; in fact, some evidence suggests that they are extremely sensitive electroreceptors that allow the animal to detect the electric field generated by its prey in water. This mole's sides and back are black to blackish brown with a paler underside. The tail is long, covered sparsely with coarse black hairs, scaly and stores fat for breeding. The tail is constricted where it meets the body. The fur is short and velvety to allow for minimal resistance as the animal moves through its burrows. A shared characteristic with other species of moles is the broad forefoot that possesses strong claws. The eyes are minute and the ears are hidden in the fur.

◆ **STATUS & HABITAT**—The star-nosed mole is a relatively common

© Dwight Kuhn

© Dwight Kuhn

The mole's sensitive nose.

mole in the southern Appalachian Mountains. It prefers wet areas in meadows, forests, or fields. It is also found in swamps, bogs, marshes, and along slow moving streams with mucky bottoms. This animal is not commonly observed since it spends most of its time underground. In the Americas this mole occurs from the Atlantic coast of Canada to eastern Manitoba. Its range extends south to Minnesota, northern Indiana, and along the Appalachian Mountains to north Georgia and South Carolina. It is not found in the piedmont but does occur along the Atlantic coast to Georgia.

Favorite star-nosed mole meals include terrestrial and aquatic earthworms, insects, leeches, mollusks, crustaceans, and fish. This species is prey for skunks, mink, snakes, and birds of prey. As many as

10 to 15 moles can be found per acre in exceptional habitat. This species helps to till and aerate the soil. Usually three to seven young are born per litter and these young can in turn breed when they are ten months old. Usually one litter is produced per year.

These moles are both nocturnal and diurnal. They form both sub-surface burrows and surface runway systems. The star-nosed mole spends more time on the surface than the other two species of eastern moles. It is also the most aquatic of the moles and is an excellent swimmer. It forages in the water and constructs burrow systems that open underwater. Nests (five to six inch diameters) of dried leaves and grass are constructed just below the surface under logs, stumps, or roots.

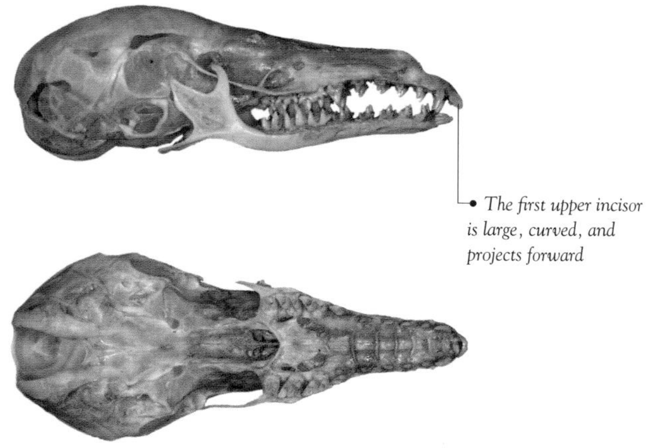

The first upper incisor is large, curved, and projects forward

Bats

ORDER CHIROPTERA

Family Vespertilionidae

Little Brown Bat
Northern Long-eared Bat
Indiana Bat
Eastern Small-footed Bat
Silver-haired Bat
Eastern Pipistrelle
Big Brown Bat
Eastern Red Bat
Hoary Bat
Rafinesque's Big-eared Bat
Evening Bat
Seminole Bat
Gray Bat

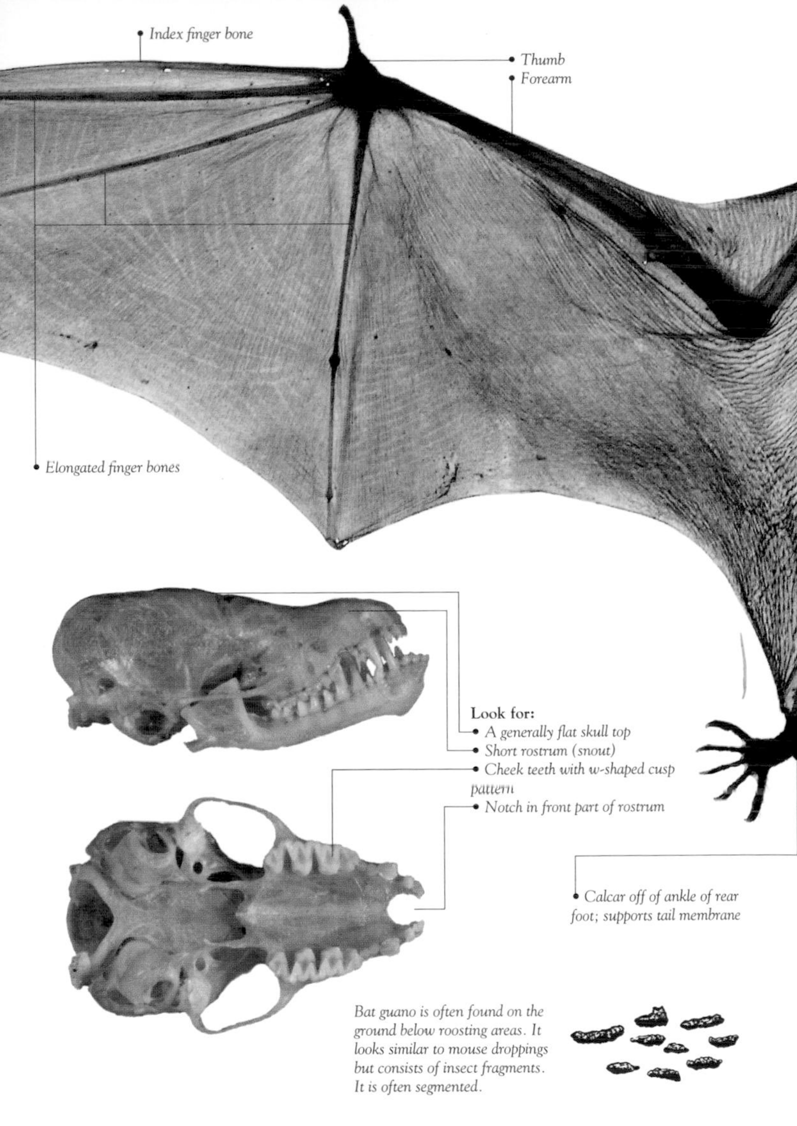

Bat guano is often found on the ground below roosting areas. It looks similar to mouse droppings but consists of insect fragments. It is often segmented.

Little Brown Bat

J. Scott Altenbach

Myotis lucifugus

3″ - 3 7/10″ length
(75 - 95 mm)

8 7/10″ - 10 3/5″ wingspan
(220 - 272 mm)

1/5 - 3/10 oz
(5 - 9 g)

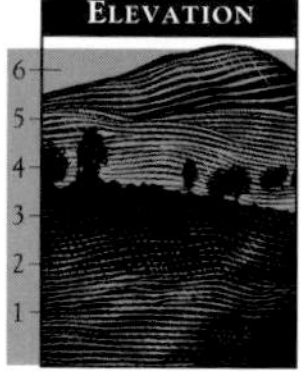

The little brown bat, or little brown myotis, is a medium-sized bat, usually with glossy brown fur. The ventral surface is usually lighter, more of a buff color. Long hairs on the feet extend beyond the tips of the toes. The tragus is medium sized and rounded. The calcar is usually not keeled, but some exhibit a slight keel. It can easily be confused with other members of the genus *Myotis*, especially the Indiana bat, because of similarities of appearance. However, the Indiana bat has slightly smaller feet, has a keel on the calcar, does not have long hairs on the foot extending beyond the tips of the toes, and the fur is dull, not glossy.

◆ **STATUS & HABITAT**—During summer, little brown bats often inhabit buildings where females form nursery colonies, sometimes numbering hundreds or even thousands of individuals. Those inhabiting wooded areas often roost in hollow trees. Males appear to be more solitary and sometimes roost in caves during summer. This species, and the big brown bat, are the two bats that are most often found roosting in buildings in the park and elsewhere throughout their ranges. Little brown bats are relatively common in the Smokies.

During winter, little brown bats hibernate in caves and mines, usually in warmer areas than those chosen by most other members of the genus *Myotis*. They may be found clustered together, or scattered and hanging singly. Several hundred usually hibernate in White Oak Blowhole Cave in the park. A few hibernate in other park caves. Only nine caves are present in the park, all in a limestone area in the northwestern section.

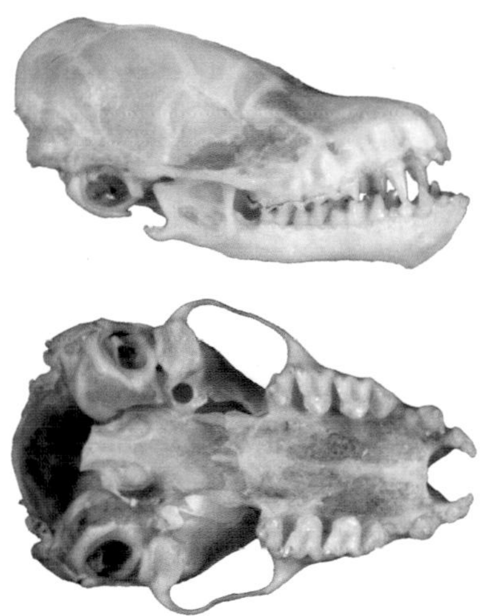

This species seems to prefer foraging over water, but also forages among trees in rather open areas. Food includes gnats, mosquitoes, flies, beetles, wasps, and moths. Mating occurs in autumn, but may also occur during the hibernation period. One pup is born, usually between late May and early July. Young develop rapidly and are capable of flight within about three weeks. Like other hibernating bat species, young have a limited amount of time to learn to catch insects and to build up the necessary fat reserves to survive the hibernation period. A lifespan of over 30 years has been recorded for this species.

Nearly all United States bat species, and 70% of bats worldwide, feed almost exclusively on insects. In fact, bats are the only major predators of night-flying insects. Bats usually eat more than 50% of their body weight in insects each night.

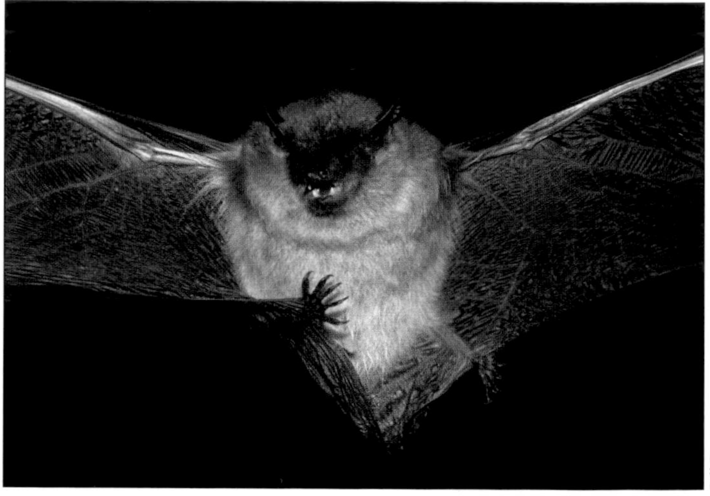

Bill Beatty

Northern Long-eared Bat

Myotis septentrionalis
3″ - 3 1/2″ length
(77 - 90 mm)

8 9/10″ - 10 1/5″ wingspan
(226 - 260 mm)

1/5 - 2/5 oz
(5 - 10 g)

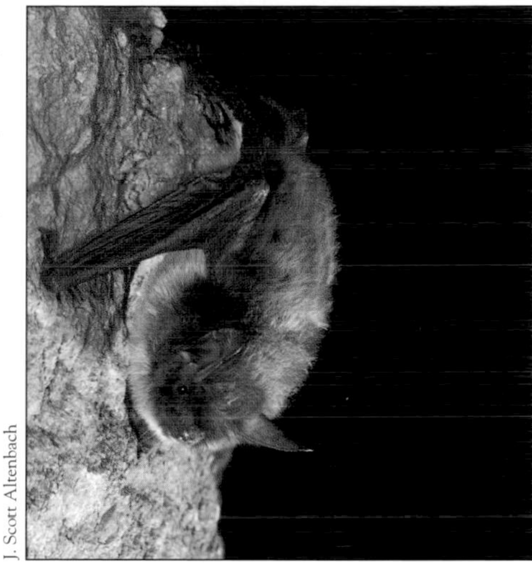

J. Scott Altenbach

The northern long-eared bat, also known as northern long-eared myotis or northern myotis, is a medium-sized bat with long ears (when compared to most other members of the very large genus *Myotis*). It has brown pelage, which is dull, not glossy, a long, sharp-pointed tragus, and the calcar is not keeled. It can be confused with other members of the genus *Myotis* because of similarities in appearance. However, the longer ears and long, sharp-pointed tragus distinguish it from other park *Myotis*.

◆ **STATUS & HABITAT**—During summer these bats roost in a variety of shelters, including buildings, hollow trees, and under loose tree bark. This species appears to be more solitary than other *Myotis*, and they generally roost singly or in small groups. Although they frequently hang in the open, they seem to prefer tight crevices and holes.

Mating occurs in August and September, when this species can be found swarming at cave entrances with other bat species. A single pup is born in June or July. Northern long-eared bats have been known to live for more than 18 years.

Until recently this species, along with a separate population in the northwestern United States and Canada, was called Keen's bat or Keen's myotis, *Myotis keenii*. It has now been determined that the two populations represent different species. Thus, the northwestern species retains the name *Myotis keenii*, while the eastern species is now known as *Myotis septentrionalis*.

Although bats have relatively good eyesight, most depend on their well-developed echolocation (or sonar) ability to navigate and capture insects in the dark. Bats emit pulses of very high frequency

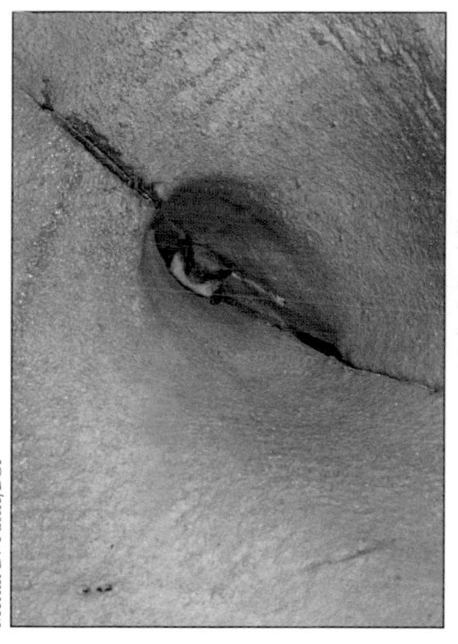
Merlin D. Tuttle/BCI

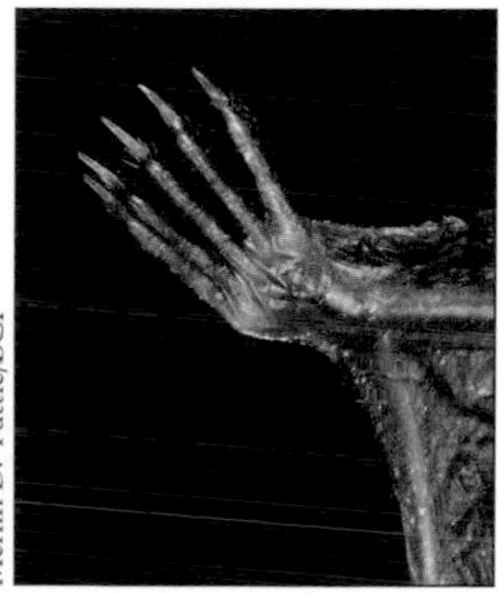
Merlin D. Tuttle/BCI

This species tends to roost singly or in small groups.

sound (too high for humans to hear) at a rate of up to 200 per second.

Northern long-eared bats forage mainly on forested hillsides and ridges, usually relatively low above the ground. This species feeds on a variety of insects, including moths, flies, beetles, and caddisflies. They are also known to consume spiders. Northern long-eared bats are relatively common in the park, although the park is near the southern edge of their range. This species is usually considered to be a "northern bat," but it has recently been found to be relatively abundant in Tennessee, North Carolina, Kentucky, and Arkansas.

Northern long-eared bats hibernate in caves and mines, usually in areas that are relatively cool and moist. Some can be observed hanging from cave ceilings, but most are well hidden in cracks and crevices.

The northern long-eared bat is listed as a species of special concern by the North Carolina Wildlife Resources Commission.

Indiana Bat

J. Scott Altenbach

Myotis sodalis
Endangered

2 4/5" - 3 7/10" length
(71 - 93 mm)

9 1/2" - 10 3/5"
wingspan
(240 - 270 mm)

1/5 - 3/10 oz
(5 - 9 g)

The Indiana bat, or Indiana myotis, is a medium-sized bat with dull grayish fur above and somewhat lighter fur below. The pelage is faintly tri-colored; hairs are black at the base, grayish in the middle, and brown at the tip. The fur is dull, not glossy. The calcar is keeled and the tragus is short and rounded. Hairs on the feet do not extend beyond the tips of the toes. It can easily be confused with other members of the genus *Myotis*, especially the little brown bat, because of similarities in general appearance. However, the little brown bat has slightly larger feet, lacks a keel on the calcar, has long hairs on

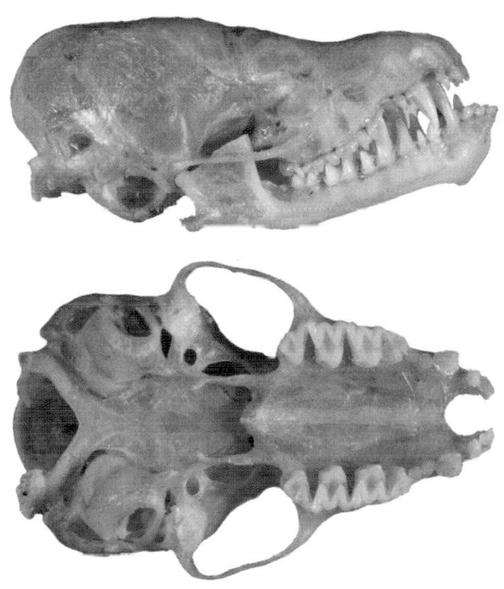

the feet extending beyond the tips of the toes, and has a glossy sheen to the fur.

During summer, these bats form small colonies in wooded areas where they roost primarily under loose bark of dead trees. Females form maternity colonies of a few to over 100 individuals where they raise their young. Males are more solitary. Only a few maternity colonies of this species have been discovered south of Kentucky, two of which are in the park (the others are in nearby areas of Tennessee and North Carolina).

◆ **STATUS & HABITAT**—During winter, Indiana bats hibernate in relatively cold areas of caves or mines where the temperature is generally 35-45° F. Hibernating bats form tight clusters of up to 480 bats per square foot. White Oak Blowhole Cave in the park houses the largest known Indiana bat hibernating colony south of Kentucky, usually numbering 6,000-10,000 bats. Smaller hibernating colonies numbering in the hundreds inhabit two additional park caves. The park is near the southern edge of this species' range.

Indiana bats generally forage in the forest canopy. They feed on a variety of insects, including small moths, flies, mosquitoes, and beetles. Mating occurs primarily during fall swarming at hibernation caves. Females give birth to a single pup, usually during June. Pups are weaned and begin to fly by mid July. Lifespans of nearly 20 years have been recorded.

The Indiana bat is the only bat confirmed to inhabit the park that is listed as Endangered (in danger of extinction) by the U.S. Fish and Wildlife Service and the National Park Service. White Oak Blowhole Cave is listed as critical habitat for the species and has been gated to prevent human disturbance to the hibernating colony. Awakening hibernating bats results in significant loss of fat reserves, necessary for survival through the winter. Range-wide, Indiana bat populations have declined drastically during the past 40 years, in spite of recovery efforts. However, recent increases have been observed, especially in the Midwest and Northeast.

Merlin D. Tuttle/BCI

A cluster of Indiana bats awakens from hibernation.

Eastern Small-footed Bat

Myotis leibii

2 4/5" - 3 3/10" length
(72 - 83 mm)

8 3/10" - 9 1/2" wingspan
(210 - 240 mm)

1/10 - 1/5 oz
(3 - 6 g)

J. Scott Altenbach

The eastern small-footed bat is one of the smallest bats in the United States and the smallest bat inhabiting the park. Its fur is relatively long and is usually brown to tan in color. Its face, including nose, ears, and tragus, is black, resulting in a masked appearance. The calcar is keeled. Although it is somewhat similar in appearance to other members of the genus *Myotis*, such as the little brown bat, its small size, tiny feet, and black facial mask easily identify it.

◆ **STATUS & HABITAT**—The eastern small-footed bat appears to be one of the rarest bats in the park; only a few have been reported. During

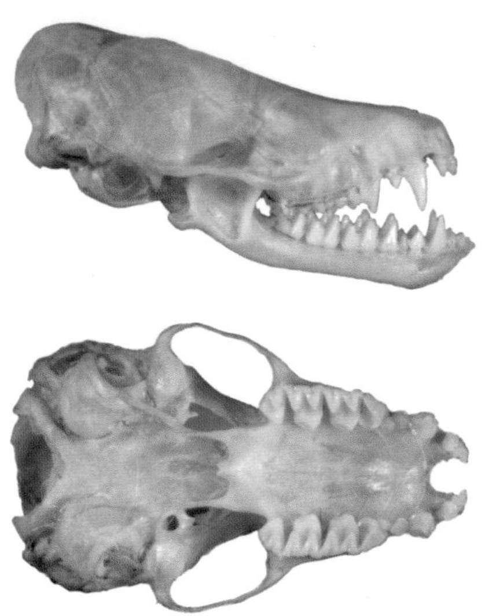

mist-netting studies in the park in the summers of 1999 and 2000, no eastern small-footed bats were netted among 258 bats captured. However, it is likely more abundant than capture records indicate. More than 30 have been observed during summer roosting in expansion joints of two high elevation highway bridges close to the park.

Little is known about the breeding habits of this species. Females give birth to one pup per season.

We also know relatively little about the summer roosting habits of this species. It has been found inhabiting buildings during summer. It has also been found under rocks on hillsides and near cave entrances, in rock and bluff cracks and crevices, and under or in expansion joints of bridges. Individuals usually are solitary, although small maternity colonies of up to 20 individuals have been reported from buildings. They eat flies, mosquitoes, true bugs, beetles, ants, and other insects.

Eastern small-footed bats hibernate in caves and mines, usually in relatively cold areas near the entrance. They usually hang singly. Their tolerance for cold, dry roost sites is remarkable for such a small bat.

Although not considered endangered or threatened, the eastern small-footed bat is listed as a federal species of concern by the U.S. Fish and Wildlife Service and National Park Service, and as a species of special concern by the North Carolina Wildlife Resources Commission. The Tennessee Wildlife Resources Agency lists it as deemed in need of management.

Although almost all United States bat species are primarily insectivorous, bats in other parts of the world feed on a variety of items in addition to insects. Many species, including the large "flying foxes," eat primarily fruit, while several species feed on nectar and pollen. A few species eat fish, which they capture by flying low over the water's surface and gaffing the fish with their exceptionally long claws. Vampire bats of Mexico, Central America, and South America feed exclusively on blood of mammals and birds, which they lick (not suck) from their victims after biting them.

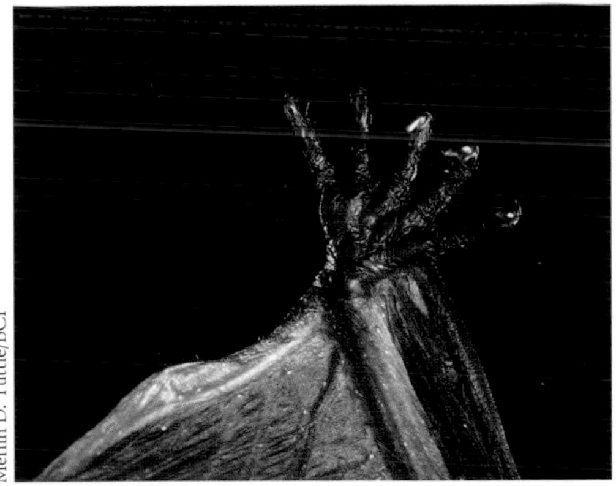

Merlin D. Tuttle/BCI

Foot showing keel on the calcar, a cartilaginous projection from the ankle that supports the tail membrane.

SILVER-HAIRED BAT

Michael Durham

Lasionycteris noctivagans

3 1/5″ - 4 2/5″ length
(90 - 112 mm)

10 6/10″ - 12 1/5″ wingspan
(270 - 310 mm)

3/10 - 1/2 oz
(7 - 15 g)

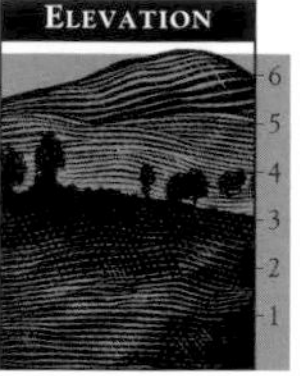

The silver-haired bat is medium sized with dark blackish-brown, silver-tipped hair. The silver-tipped hair is more pronounced along the middle of the back. The ears are short, rounded, and naked. It can be distinguished from all other bats in the park by a combination of color and its small size.

◆ **STATUS & HABITAT**—This bat is a migratory, tree dwelling species. Most spend summers well north of the park and migrate south

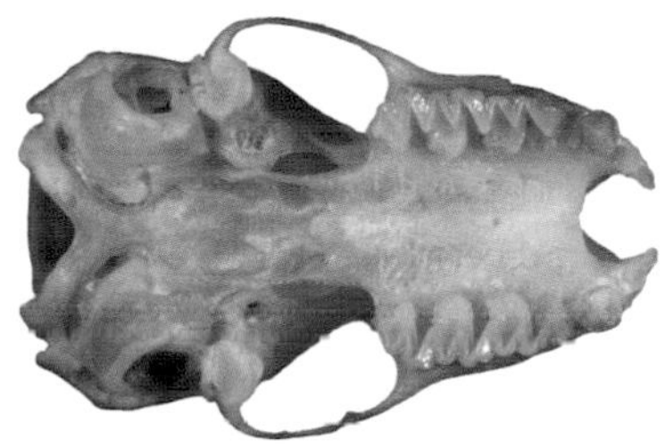

in winter. They are considered rare in the park. However, a few have been captured in the park during summer. Two were mist-netted among 258 bats captured during the summers of 1999 and 2000. They appear to be rather solitary, although small groups and small maternity colonies have been reported.

During summer, they often roost under loose tree bark, but have also been found in buildings, woodpecker holes, bird nests, and hollow trees. Silver-haired bats are known to consume a variety of insects, including moths, flies, mosquitoes, true bugs, termites, and beetles. They forage primarily over woodland ponds and streams. They are considered to be one of the slowest flying bats in North America.

Silver-haired bats hibernate throughout most of the southeastern United States. They seldom enter caves, although a few have been reported hibernating in caves and mines. They usually hibernate in trees, buildings, rock crevices, and similar habitats.

Young are apparently raised in the northern tier states and northward into Canada. Most females give birth to twins in June or July. This species appears to be relatively common throughout much of its range, but relatively uncommon in the southeastern United States.

There are over 1,100 species of bats known worldwide, and new species are occasionally still being discovered, especially in parts of the world that previously lacked intensive scientific investigation. Their greatest numbers and diversity occur in warmer latitudes. Forty-six species are known to occur in the United States; 16 in the Tennessee/ North Carolina area; 11 species have been reported in the park.

Several animals, including raccoons, skunks, owls, hawks, and snakes prey on bats, but few animals consume bats as a regular part of their diet. Humans, however, can have a significant impact on bat populations. Adverse impacts include habitat destruction, direct killing, vandalism, disturbance to hibernating and maternity colonies, and pesticide use on their food (insects).

Bats are among the most misunderstood animals in the United States. However, as consumers of enormous numbers of insects, they are extremely beneficial. Superstitions and misconceptions about them are far too numerous. They aren't blind, they aren't "flying mice," and they don't try to get entangled in human hair.

Michael Durham

EASTERN PIPISTRELLE

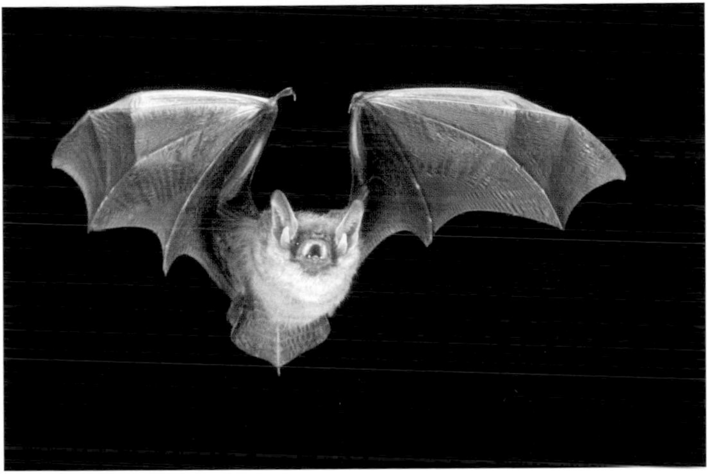

J. Scott Altenbach

Perimyotis subflavus

3″ - 3 7/10″ length
(77 - 93 mm)

8 1/5″ - 10 1/5″ wingspan
(208 - 260 mm)

1/10 - 3/10 oz
(3 - 7 g)

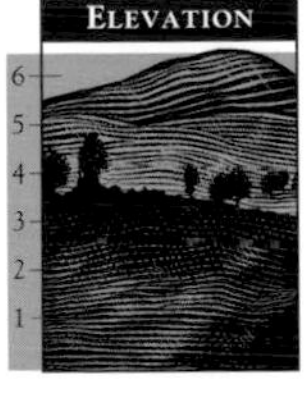

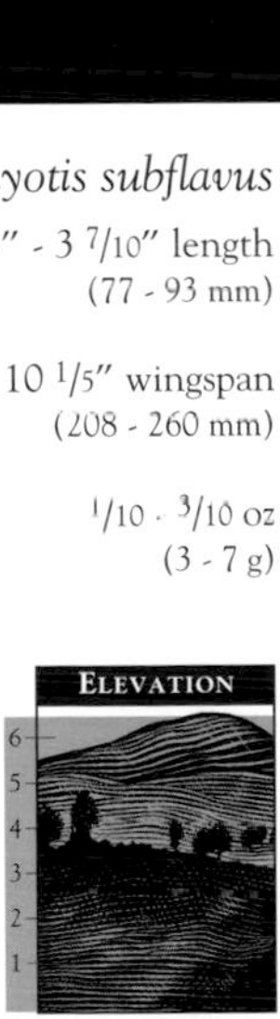

The eastern pipistrelle is one of the smallest bats living in the park. The pelage is tri-colored; hairs on the back are reddish-brown at the tip, yellowish-brown in the middle, and dark at the base. The thumb is long, about one-fifth the length of the forearm. The skin covering the forearm is pale reddish, contrasting with the darker wing membrane. The calcar is not keeled. It can be confused with some of the smaller members of the genus *Myotis*, but can be distinguished from them by its tri-colored hair, contrasting wing colors, and long thumb.

Eastern pipistrelles begin foraging early in the evening and can be distinguished by their rather erratic flight pattern, resembling that of a large moth. They eat a variety of insects, including moths, beetles, mosquitoes, true bugs, and ants.

Mating occurs in autumn and fertilization is delayed until spring. Eastern pipistrelles usually give birth to twins during late spring or early summer. Pups are born hairless and with their eyes closed. They grow rapidly and can fly within a month after birth. The greatest longevity period recorded for this species is 14.8 years.

◆ **STATUS & HABITAT**—Eastern pipistrelles are rather common in the park. They generally roost in trees during summer; a few may be found roosting in caves or buildings. They are often solitary, but sometimes roost in small groups, especially females, which form small maternity colonies of a few to 30 or more individuals.

These bats hibernate in caves or mines. They inhabit more caves in eastern North America than any other bat species, usually hanging singly in warmer parts of the cave. Several hundred usually hibernate in Gregory Cave in Cades Cove. That cave has been gated to protect eastern pipistrelles, as well as other bats, from disturbance during hibernation. This is the only bat species that can usually be found hibernating in all nine park caves.

To inventory park bats, researchers enter caves during winter and count hibernating bats. Tightly clustered bats are counted by measuring the area covered by clusters and multiplying by a previously determined density factor, e.g., 300 - 480 bats per square foot for Indiana bats. During summer, scientists sample various park locations using bat traps or mist-nets made of very fine thread.

Observations of bat activity are also made using night-vision scopes and with ultrasonic bat detectors, devices that render ultrasonic bat cries audible to human ears or that produce sonograms which can be used to identify bats down to species. Most bats captured during studies are also banded with numbered wing bands.

Robert and Linda Mitchell

BIG BROWN BAT

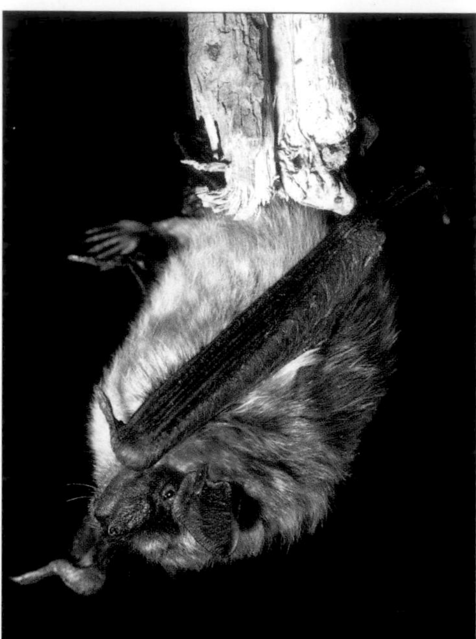

© Dwight Kuhn

Eptesicus fuscus

3 9/10″ - 5 1/10″ length
(100 - 130 mm)

12 6/10″ - 14 6/10″ wingspan
(320 - 370 mm)

5/10 - 8/10 oz
(13 - 23 g)

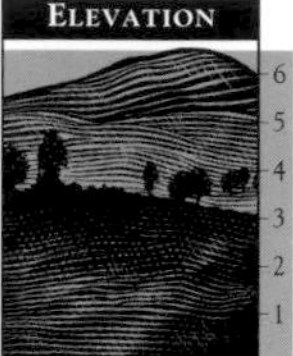

The big brown bat is the second largest bat inhabiting the park; the hoary bat is slightly larger. The big brown bat's color varies from dark brown to a lighter brown; hair on the ventral surface is somewhat lighter. It has broad wings and a keeled calcar. This species and the evening bat are very similar in appearance, but the big brown bat is much larger.

◆ **STATUS & HABITAT**—Big brown bats occupy a variety of habitats during summer, including hollow trees and buildings. This species, and the little brown bat, are the two bats that are most often found roosting in buildings in the park, as well as throughout most of their ranges. They are relatively common in the Smokies; summer colonies inhabit several buildings scattered throughout the park. Females form summer maternity colonies of a few to several hundred individuals. Males hang separately, often in the same roost structure.

Where most big brown bats hibernate is not known, although many hibernate in caves, mines, and buildings. Many likely hibernate in hollow trees. A few are usually found hibernating in the larger caves in the park. They usually choose hibernation sites that are relatively cold.

This species has one of the largest distributions of any North American bat, covering most of the 48 contiguous states, southern Canada, and into South America.

Left: bat ear showing tragus. Right: wing showing thumb (first digit).

© Dwight Kuhn

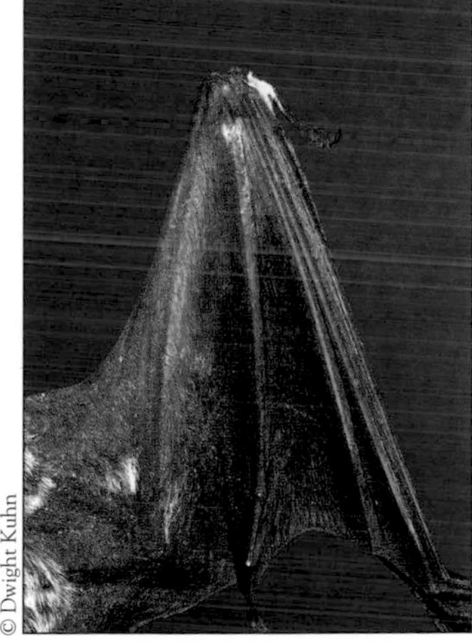

© Dwight Kuhn

Mating occurs in autumn and winter, and fertilization is delayed until spring. In the park and throughout the eastern United States big brown bats usually give birth to twins, while in the western part of their range only one pup is born. Birth occurs during late May and early June. Pups develop rapidly and are weaned when about four weeks old. By the age of two months, they are almost as large as their parents.

Big brown bats feed on a variety of insects, including beetles, flies, mosquitoes, mayflies, and ants. They seem to prefer larger prey items, when available. Like many other bat species, they often fly to a night roost after feeding, where they rest before feeding again later in the night. Many big brown bats live for at least 10 years; the longest known longevity for this species is 19 years.

A few eastern United States bat species, like the big brown bat and little brown bat, given the opportunity, may take up residence in attics or other parts of buildings. Most people prefer not to share their dwellings with colonies of bats. The best method of preventing bats from roosting in houses or other buildings is by simply closing openings through which they enter. Small man-made bat houses designed to attract bats have become popular with the public during recent years.

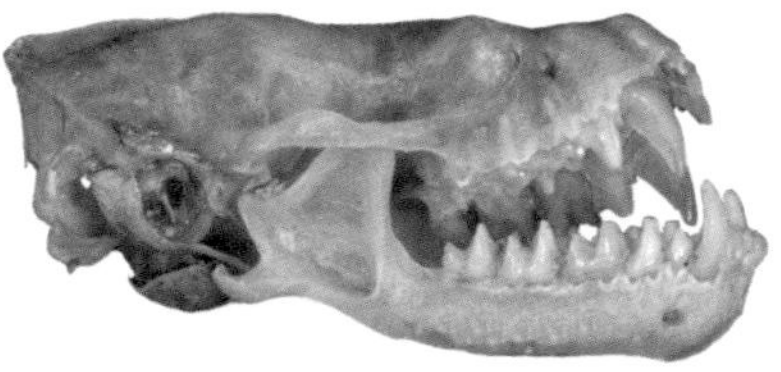

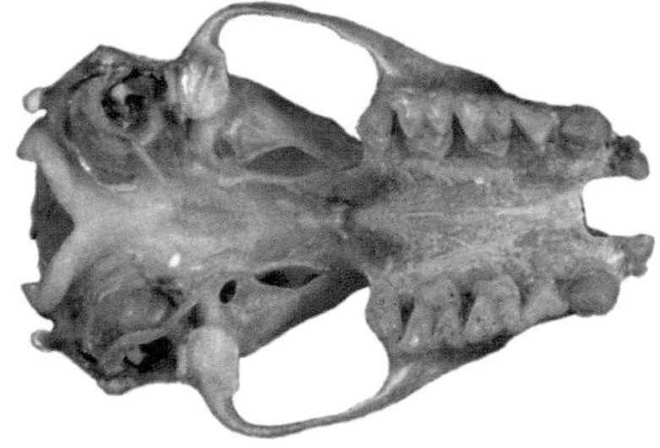

Eastern Red Bat

Lasiurus borealis

3 7/10″ - 4 9/10″ length
(95 - 125 mm)

11 1/5″ - 13″ wingspan
(285 - 330 mm)

3/10 - 1/2 oz
(9 - 15 g)

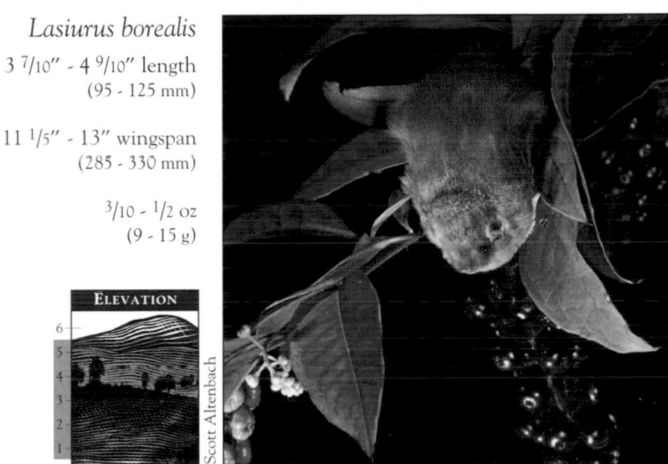

J. Scott Altenbach

The eastern red bat has long pointed wings and short rounded ears. The body is almost completely furred, except for the ears and parts of the wings. The tail membrane is heavily furred. It is one of only a very few mammals in which color varies between males and females. Males are usually more brightly colored than females; bright orange-red with a frosted effect due to the white tips of the hair. Females are dull yellow-brown with similar white frosting. Both sexes have a white patch on each shoulder. The tragus is less than one-half the length of the ear, is curved forward, and is broad at the base, tapering to a slightly rounded tip. The calcar is keeled.

This species, especially females, could most easily be confused with the Seminole bat, which is usually a darker mahogany brown, or with the hoary bat, which is gray and larger. Seminole bats have not been reported in the park, but are likely present, since they have been reported from similar habitats nearby.

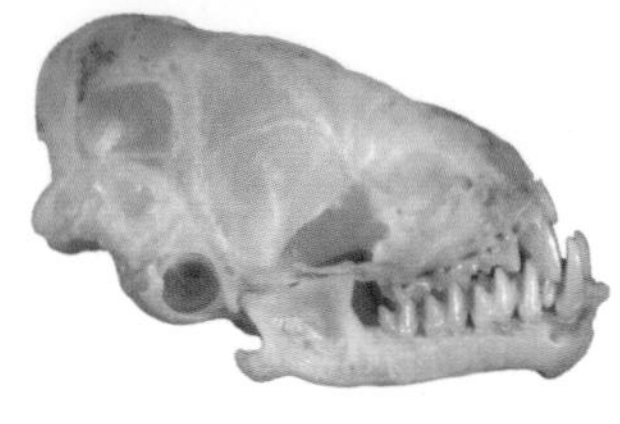

Until relatively recently this species was called simply the red bat. However, it was determined that the eastern and western populations are distinct species. Thus, the species present in the park is now known as the eastern red bat, although its scientific name has not changed.

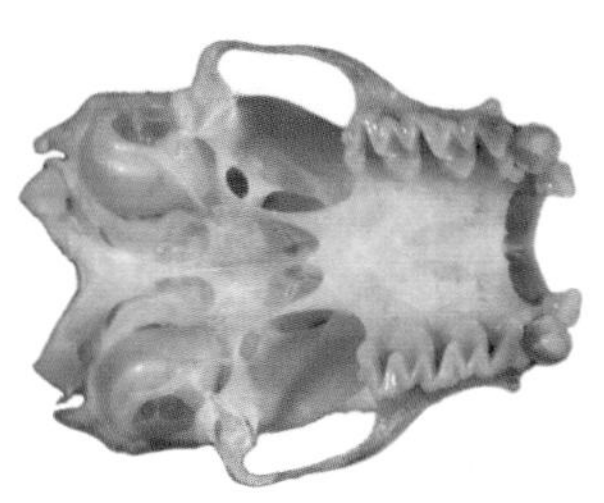

◆ **STATUS & HABITAT**—The eastern red bat is a tree bat, seldom entering caves, although they often swarm around cave entrances during autumn. They are relatively abundant throughout the park. This species is solitary and daylight hours are spent hanging in the foliage of trees or shrubs. They usually hang by one foot, giving the appearance of dead leaves. They emerge early in the evening and forage on a variety of insects, including moths, flies, mosquitoes, true bugs, beetles, and cicadas. They often forage over the same territory on successive nights. Eastern red bats, as well as other bat species, are frequently seen feeding around lights, which attract large numbers of insects.

During winter, eastern red bats usually hibernate in hollow trees or on the ground in leaf litter. Some may migrate to warmer climates. They are often observed flying on warm winter afternoons.

Bats detect flying insects by echolocation and usually capture them by scooping them into their tail or wing membranes, then taking them into their mouths. This results in the erratic flight often observed while they are feeding on insects. A single bat feeding on small insects may capture and consume more than 3,000 insects in a single night. Bats drink by skimming close to the surface of a body of water and gulping an occasional mouthful.

Hoary Bat

Michael Durham

Lasiurus cinereus

4″ - 5 9/10″ length
(102 - 150 mm)

13 8/10″ - 16 1/10″ wingspan
(350 - 410 mm)

7/10 - 1 3/10 oz
(20 - 38 g)

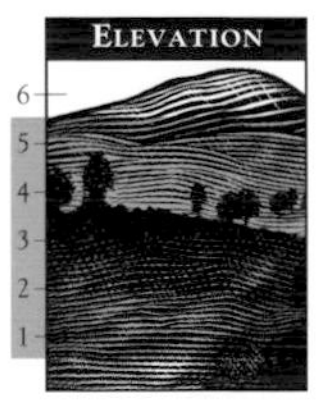

The hoary bat is the largest bat inhabiting the park, and is the most widespread bat occurring in the Americas, ranging from southern Canada southward through much of South America. It is the only native land mammal in Hawaii. The hoary bat is heavily furred. Tips of many of the hairs are white, giving an overall frosted, or hoary, appearance. The ears are relatively short and rounded and edged with black. It is not easily confused with any other American bat, with the possible exception of the silver-haired bat, which is much smaller and not as heavily furred.

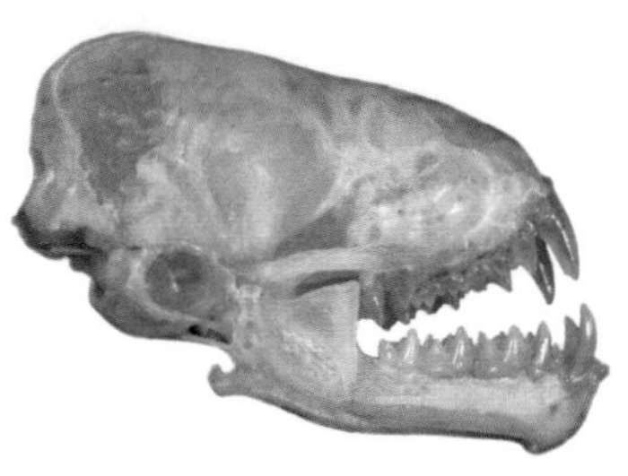
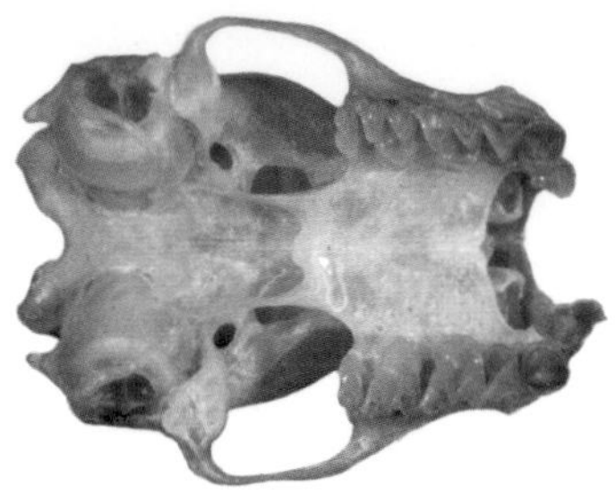

◆ **STATUS & HABITAT**—Northern populations make long seasonal migrations to and from warmer winter habitats. They appear to be rather rare in the park; summer mist-netting in 1999 and 2000 resulted in the capture of only five specimens among 258 bats caught. The hoary bat is a tree bat, seldom entering caves. They have rarely been found in buildings. They are solitary and roost in the foliage of trees where they are usually well hidden during daytime. Because of their relative rarity, especially in the eastern United States, along with the fact that they seldom enter caves or buildings, they are not often encountered by humans.

Hoary bats feed on a wide variety of insects, including beetles, flies, and true bugs, but seem to prefer large moths. They have been observed pursuing other bats, and may sometimes capture and eat smaller bats, such as eastern pipistrelles.

Like most bats of the family *Vespertilionidae*, to which all park species belong, mating probably occurs primarily during autumn and fertilization is delayed until late winter or early spring. Female hoary bats usually give birth to two pups, which are born in late May, June, or early July. Pups cling to their mother during the day, but are left in the foliage at night while she leaves to forage. Young grow rapidly, and are able to fly and care for themselves within about a month after birth.

Although the hoary bat is the most widespread of American bats, relatively little is known about its particular habits, distribution, and numbers.

Bats are extremely long-lived for such small mammals. Most other small mammal species, such as shrews, live two years at most. Bats, however, often live 10-15 years or more. Life spans of over 30 years have been recorded. Longevity records have resulted from marking and recapturing individuals during many years of bat research. Much of what is known about bat biology, such as movements and migrations, has resulted from banding studies.

J. Scott Altenbach

Michael Durham

Rafinesque's Big-eared Bat

J. Scott Altenbach

Corynorhinus rafinesquii

3 6/10" - 4 1/10" length (91 - 105 mm)

10 4/10" - 11 9/10" wingspan (263 - 301 mm)

2/10 - 4/10 oz (6 - 11 g)

Until recently, the genus name of this bat was *Plecotus*. The genus is now called *Corynorhinus*, a return to the genus name it had in the past. Its common name is in honor of Constantine Samuel Rafinesque, a famous early naturalist who was on the faculty of Transylvania University in Lexington, Kentucky.

Rafinesque's big-eared bat is a medium-sized bat with huge ears measuring more than an inch in length. Its fur is grayish brown to gray above and gray to nearly white below. It has two large lumps on its snout. Because of its large ears, it could not be confused with any other bat found in the park. However, it could be confused with the endangered

Virginia big-eared bat, *Corynorhinus townsendii virginianus*, a subspecies of Townsend's big-eared bat, which has been reported from northwestern North Carolina, but not from Tennessee or from the park. The Virginia big-eared bat is brown to blackish brown, with a brown to buff ventral surface.

◆ **STATUS & HABITAT**—During summer, Rafinesque's big-eared bats often inhabit buildings where females form maternity colonies of a few to several dozen adults. They may also roost and raise young in hollow trees, as well as in caves and mines. During winter, they usually hibernate in caves or mines, where they hang singly or clustered together. The largest known summer and winter colonies of this species occupy abandoned copper mines in the southwestern region of the park. Between 1,000 and 1,500 hibernating Rafinesque's big-eared bats may be present there. Individuals or small numbers of these bats are often found in park buildings during summer.

Rafinesque's big-eared bat is listed as a federal species of concern by the U.S. Fish and Wildlife Service and the National Park Service. The North Carolina Wildlife Resources Commission lists it as a threatened species and the Tennessee Wildlife Resources Agency lists it as deemed in need of management.

These bats usually emerge from their daytime roosts late in the

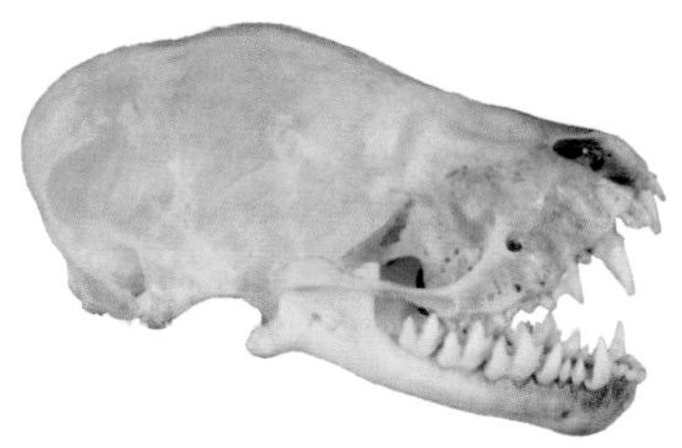

evening to forage. Their flight is remarkably agile. Moths are their preferred food, making up over 90% of their diet. Mating occurs during autumn and winter; fertilization is delayed until spring. A single pup is born in late May or early June. Pups are capable of flight at about three weeks of age.

During bat hibernation, normal metabolic activities are greatly reduced. Body temperature is reduced from over 100° F to that of the hibernation site, usually 40-60° F. The heart rate is slowed from over 1,000 beats per minute (bat in flight) to only one beat every four or five seconds. A hibernating bat can thus survive on only a few grams of stored fat during their five to six month hibernation period.

Merlin D. Tuttle/BCI

Tragus of Rafinesque's big-eared bat.

Evening Bat

Nycticeius humeralis

3 2/5″ - 3 4/5″ length
(89 - 96 mm)

10 1/5″ - 11 1/5″ wingspan
(260 - 285 mm)

1/5 - 1/2 oz
(6 - 14 g)

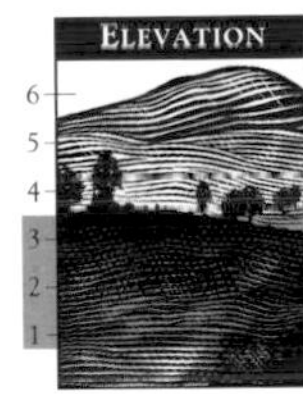

J. Scott Altenbach

The evening bat is a small brown bat, lacking distinctive external features. The fur is short and sparse and is dull brown above, and paler below. The tragus is short, curved, and rounded, and the calcar lacks a keel. This species closely resembles the big brown bat, but is considerably smaller. Length of the forearm (1.3-1.5″ or 33-39 mm) alone will distinguish the two. It somewhat resembles members of the genus *Myotis*, but its short, rounded tragus and short, sparse fur, distinguish it. It also has only one upper incisor on each side of the mouth, while *Myotis* have two.

◆ **STATUS & HABITAT**—This species appears to be one of the rarest bats inhabiting the park and has been recorded from only one section of the park, at low elevations at the western edge. It was first captured in the park during summer 1999, and was the only mammal

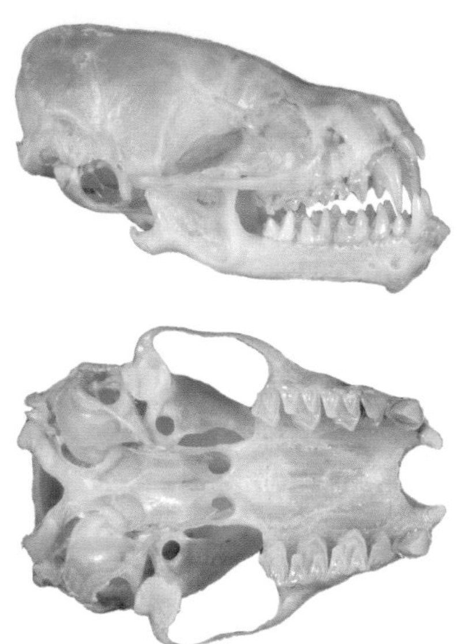

species discovered new to the park in over a decade. Although its range covers the entire southeastern United States, it is apparently relatively uncommon in the southern Appalachians.

This species usually roosts in tree cavities or buildings during summer. It seldom enters caves, although it sometimes joins other bats swarming about cave entrances in late summer. Maternity colonies in buildings sometimes contain hundreds of individuals. Smaller colonies often occur in hollow trees and under loose tree bark. The winter range of this species is almost completely unknown, although a few have been reported from Florida. Evening bats are known to accumulate large fat reserves in autumn, sufficient for either hibernation or a long migration.

Feeding habits of evening bats are not well known. However, a

Rolf Nussbaumer

colony of evening bats studied in Indiana consumed primarily beetles, moths, and leafhoppers. It was estimated that the colony of 300 bats ate about 6.3 million insects per year.

Evening bats give birth to twins between late May and mid June. Females nurse their own pups during the first two weeks following birth, then will nurse any young that approach them until weaning time. Pups can fly at about three weeks of age.

Bats, like many other mammals, can contract and transmit rabies as well as other diseases. Rabies has been found in many species of bats in the U.S., but is relatively uncommon. Rabid bats seldom are aggressive. During the past 40 years, an average of about one person per year in the United States is known to have contracted rabies from bats.

Seminole Bat

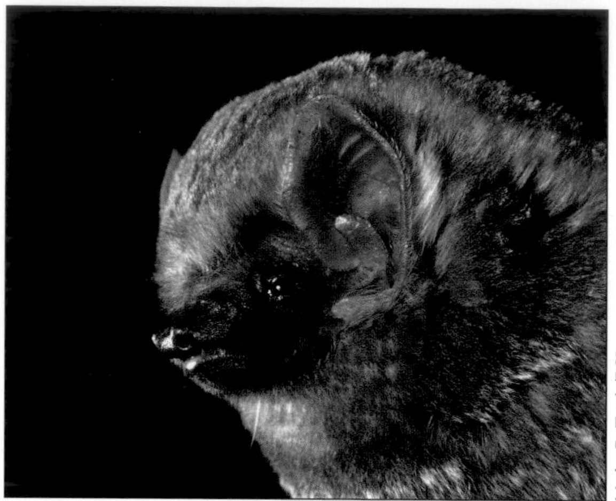

Merlin D. Tuttle/BCI

Lasiurus seminolus

3 9/10″ - 4 7/10″ length
(100 - 120 mm)

11 2/5″ - 12 3/5″
wingspan
(290 - 320 mm)

3/10 - 1/2 oz
(8 - 15 g)

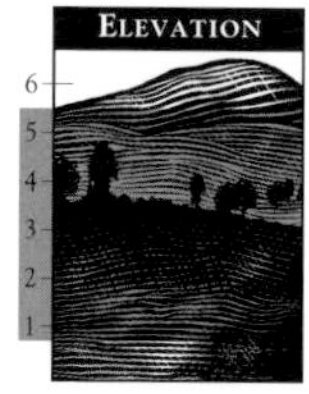

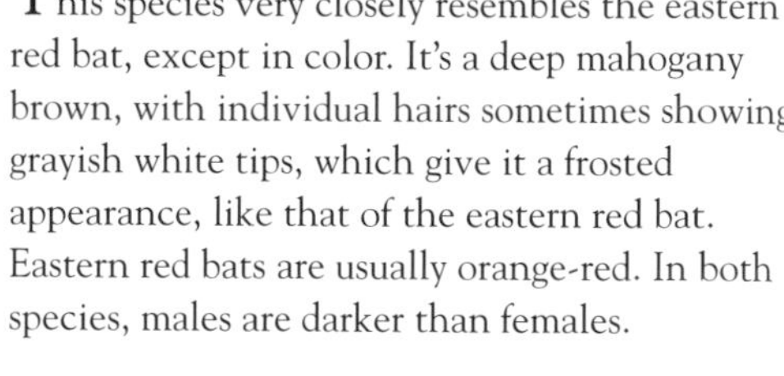

This species very closely resembles the eastern red bat, except in color. It's a deep mahogany brown, with individual hairs sometimes showing grayish white tips, which give it a frosted appearance, like that of the eastern red bat. Eastern red bats are usually orange-red. In both species, males are darker than females.

◆ **STATUS & HABITAT**—The Seminole bat has not been reported from the park, but it is likely present. It has been reported from within 15 miles of the western park boundary, at an elevation of over 4,500 feet in the Cherokee National Forest, Monroe County, Tennessee. A bat thought to be a Seminole was captured at a

Gatlinburg motel in 1993, but was released before a positive identification could be made. The Seminole bat ranges across most of the Southern states, from Tennessee and North Carolina south to the Gulf Coast and Florida and west to Texas. It is relatively abundant throughout most of its range.

Seminole bats usually give birth to two, three, or four pups during late May or June. Young are able to fly in about three weeks.

The Seminole bat is a solitary tree bat, seldom entering caves. Throughout much of the southeastern United States, Seminole bats often roost in Spanish moss. In areas where Spanish moss is not present, they roost in the foliage of trees, much like their close relative, the eastern red bat. They fly during all seasons, even on warm evenings in mid-winter. They emerge early in the evening and forage at treetop level. They are swift flyers.

Information concerning food habits of this species is rather limited. Seminole bats have been reported to eat flies, mosquitoes, beetles, true

Merlin D. Tuttle/BCI

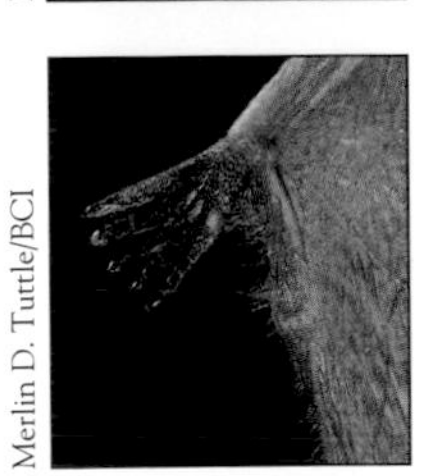

Merlin D. Tuttle/BCI

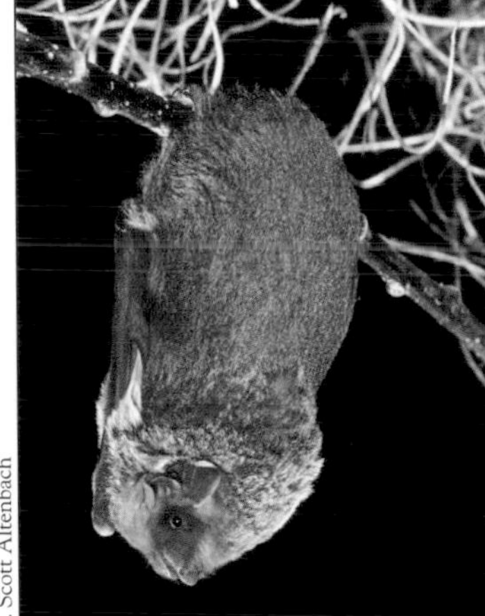

J. Scott Altenbach

Left top: tail membrane. Left bottom: foot and wing membrane.

bugs, and other insects. They may occasionally feed on the ground.

Seminole bats apparently range extensively, especially during late summer. Although outside their normal range, they have been reported from several areas to the north, including New York, Pennsylvania, Wisconsin, Indiana, Virginia, and Kentucky. This is also true for other bat species. There are records of Brazilian free-tailed bats, for example, from several locations outside their normal range, including a record from west Tennessee. However, it is not considered by most to be a Tennessee mammal. The term "accidental" is often used to describe distributional records outside the normal range.

All United States bats are relatively small when compared to many species in other parts of the world. Worldwide, bats vary in size from slightly over two grams (0.07 oz), to more than three pounds. The large "flying foxes" of Africa, Australia, Asia, and many Pacific islands may have a wingspan of up to six feet.

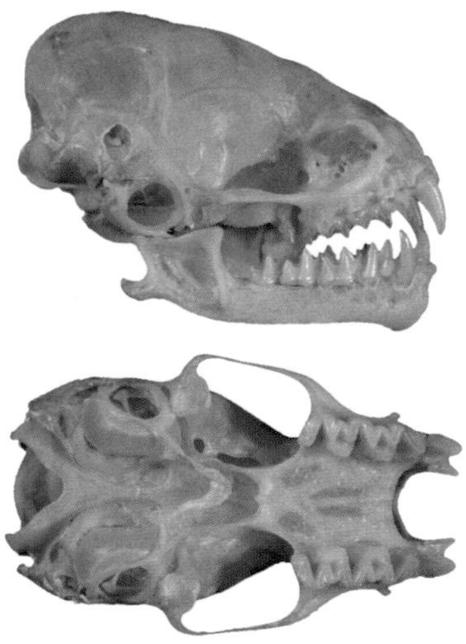

Myotis grisescens
Endangered

3 1/5" - 3 4/5" length
(80 - 96 mm)

10 4/5" - 12" wingspan
(275 - 305 mm)

3/10 - 2/5 oz
(7 - 11 g)

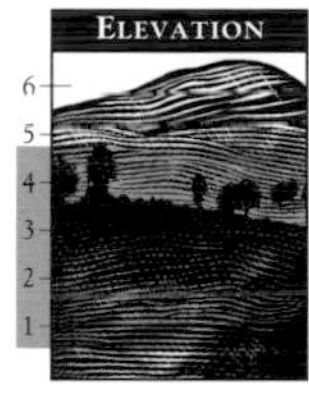

Merlin D. Tuttle/BCI

The gray bat is a large, big-footed *Myotis*, larger than any of the four *Myotis* species known in the park. Its color is uniformly gray, occasionally brownish. The calcar is not keeled. The wing membrane is attached to the foot at the ankle, instead of at the base of the toes as in other *Myotis* species. That, along with size and color, distinguishes it from other *Myotis* inhabiting the park.

◆ **STATUS & HABITAT**—The gray bat has not been reported from the park, but may be present, especially in the northeastern section. Several thousand hibernate, and smaller numbers roost during summer, in a Cocke County, Tennessee cave, less than 15 miles northeast of the park. Gray bats often fly greater distances than that from their roost sites to forage.

Gray bats are cave residents year-round, but different caves usually are occupied in summer and winter. They hibernate primarily in deep vertical caves with large rooms that act as cold air traps. More than 800,000 hibernate in four Tennessee caves. During summer, females form maternity colonies of a few hundred to many thousands of individuals in warmer caves. Males gather together and form bachelor colonies, usually in different caves than those used by females. Because of their specific habitat requirements, fewer than five percent of available caves are suitable for gray bats. Gray bats primarily forage over rivers, lakes, and large ponds. They eat moths, beetles, flies, mosquitoes, mayflies, and other insects.

Mating occurs during autumn and fertilization is delayed until spring. One pup is born in late May or early June, and is capable of flight within 20-25 days. Lifespan may exceed 15 years.

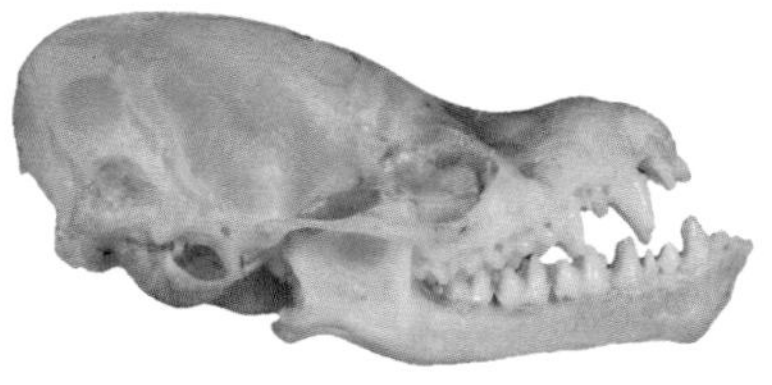

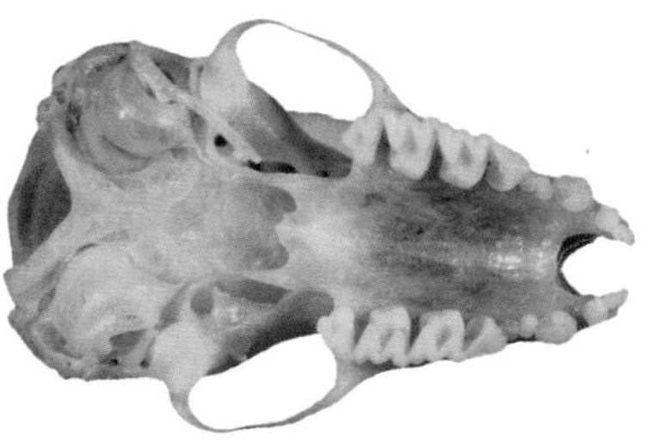

The gray bat is the only eastern U.S. bat that regularly inhabits caves in large numbers during summer. As a result, they deposit large amounts of guano (excrement) in caves they inhabit. Bat guano is an excellent fertilizer and much has been removed from caves for that purpose. During the Civil War, guano and nitrogen-rich earth were taken from numerous gray bat caves by the Confederate army and used to produce saltpeter (potassium nitrate) for use in manufacturing gunpowder. Remains of these saltpeter

Top: J. Scott Altenbach; Bottom: Merlin D. Tuttle/BCI

operations can be found in many Southeastern caves.

The gray bat is listed as Endangered by the U.S. Fish and Wildlife Service and the National Park Service. Numerous caves throughout the range of the gray bat have been gated to protect colonies from human disturbance. During recent years the gray bat recovery effort has resulted in significant population increases.

Rabbits

ORDER LAGOMORPHA

Family Leporidae

Eastern cottontail
Appalachian cottontail

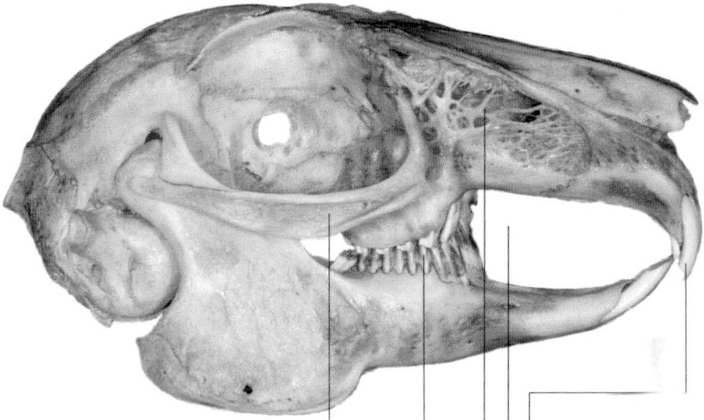

Look for:

- *Four upper incisors—two large forward incisors with two small peg incisors located in back*
- *Diastema—a space that is normally occupied by canines and premolars*
- *Fenestration—an area on the rostrum with thin, lattice-like bone*
- *Cheek teeth*
- *Zygomatic Arch—two cheekbones to which the masseter muscle attaches. The masseter muscle is a jaw-closing muscle that is well-developed in herbivores.*

Tracks follow a bounding pattern.

Cottontail rabbit scat is pellet-shaped and roughly 1/4" in diameter.

Eastern Cottontail

© Dwight Kuhn

Sylvilagus floridanus

12 3/5" - 19 3/5" length
(32.0 - 50.0 cm)

1 4/5 - 4 lbs
(0.8 - 1.8 kg)

The eyes of the eastern cottontail are circled by a cream colored ring and there is usually a white blaze on the forehead. This species is a medium-sized rabbit with relatively long, grayish ears. Its relative, the Appalachian cottontail, usually displays a black spot between the ears. However, the only way the eastern and Appalachian cottontails can be positively differentiated is by the skull and postorbital processes.

◆ **STATUS & HABITAT**—This species is a very abundant mammal in the park and occurs at all elevations. It is associated with open meadows, farmland, and forest edges. As the cleared land reverts to forests, preferred habitat decreases. One to eight young are born per litter and the female can breed again before the young are a day old. Four to six litters are produced per year. Some young breed at three to four months of age.

Generally these rabbits live only one to two years in the wild, though seven-year old rabbits have been reported. Populations can reach densities of eight to nine animals per acre. Eastern cottontails are the primary prey of bobcats, and are also preyed upon by skunks, weasels, mink, coyote, bear, foxes, and birds of prey.

© Dwight Kuhn

This rabbit takes its name from its distinctive tail.

In the Americas the eastern cottontail occurs from the Atlantic coast of New Hampshire westward to southeastern Montana. This cottontail's range then extends south to western Arizona, through Mexico and Central America.

Tularemia, rabbit fever, has been reported in this species. This bacterial disease can infect humans and can be contracted by handling or skinning an infected individual.

These rabbits forage on the ground seeking herbaceous plants such as clover, dandelion, grasses, vegetable crops, blackberries, and other fruit. They will also consume bark, saplings, and twigs and buds of trees and shrubs. Two types of fecal pellets are formed, one dry and brown and the other soft and green. They eat their green pellets since they contain high levels of nutrients.

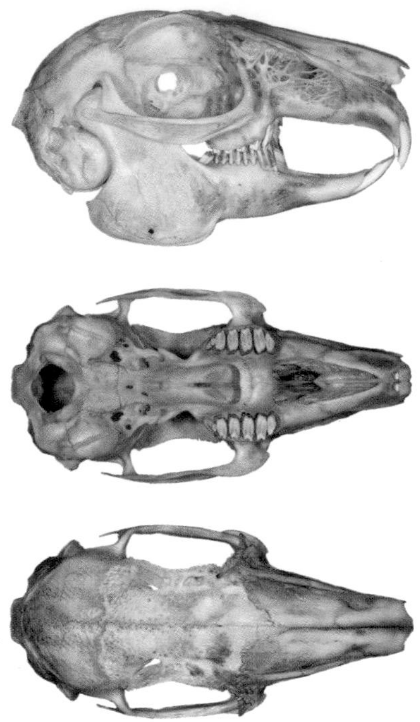

Eastern cottontails are primarily nocturnal, but can be observed at dusk and late into the morning hours. During the day this species rests in burrows constructed by other species or in dense brush. Generally this rabbit will remain still if it senses danger, but will bolt without warning at speeds of up to 10 miles per hour. Cottontails can leap 12 - 15 feet in a single bound. Their nests are usually found in shallow depressions in the ground and are lined with vegetation and fur plucked from the mother's chest and abdomen.

APPALACHIAN COTTONTAIL

Sylvilagus obscurus

13 4/5" - 17 7/10" length
(35 - 45 cm)

1 1/2 - 3 3/10 lbs
(0.7 - 1.5 kg)

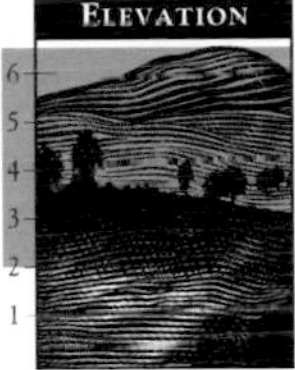

Jeffrey S. Pippen

The background color of the Appalachian cottontail's head, sides, and back is reddish to grayish brown with black hairs intermingled. The underside of the body and tail are white. Usually there is a black patch between the ears. Its ears are shorter and more rounded than the eastern cottontail's and are rimmed in black. The eastern cottontail also usually possesses a white spot or blaze on the forehead and relatively long, grayish ears. The only way that the eastern and Appalachian cottontails can be positively identified is by examination of the skull and postorbital processes.

◆ **STATUS & HABITAT**—The Appalachian cottontail has one of the most restricted distributions of any North American rabbit. Originally this species was considered to be a part of the New England cottontail group; however, chromosomal number differences have lead to the separation of these two species. As its name implies, the Appalachian cottontail occurs in the higher elevations of the Appalachian Mountains of Pennsylvania, Virginia, Kentucky, North

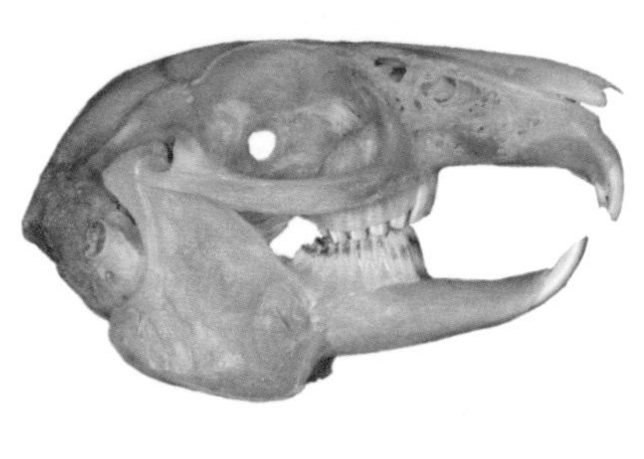

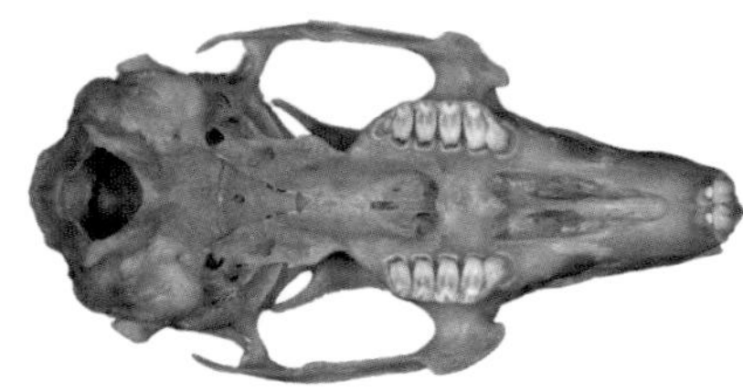

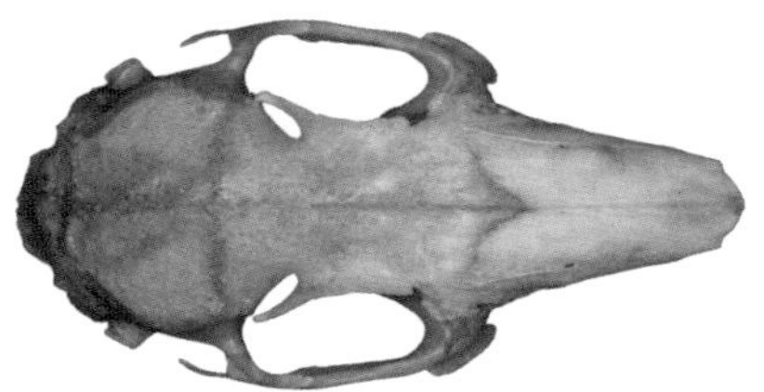

Carolina, Tennessee, Georgia, and Alabama.

The Appalachian cottontail can be found in high elevation deep coniferous forests, in yellow birch-red maple forests, in high elevation conifer and mixed forests with rhododendron thickets, and in forests with hemlock, mountain laurel, and blueberry. This species tends to avoid open meadows.

On average three to eight young are born per litter and two to four litters are produced per year. Young are altricial—born naked and require heat from the mother to maintain body temperature. They are prey for bobcats, weasels, coyote, foxes, and hawks.

Appalachian cottontails are primarily nocturnal. During the day they rest in burrows constructed by other species, in dense brush piles, or in forms found in dense vegetation. Their nests are usually found in shallow saucer-like depressions in the ground and are lined with vegetation and fur plucked from the mother's chest and abdominal areas.

This species is relatively rare in the park and occurs primarily at the higher elevations. The lack of distinguishing external characteristics makes it difficult to tell the eastern cottontail from the Appalachian. The large tracts of dense forests at high elevations provide a very important refuge for the Appalachian cottontail within the park.

These rabbits forage on the ground for herbaceous vegetation, grasses, and ferns. They will also consume bark, saplings, twigs and buds of trees and shrubs. It is considered to be the only cottontail that feeds heavily on conifer needles.

Rodents

ORDER RODENTIA

Family Sciuridae
Eastern Chipmunk
Woodchuck
Eastern Gray Squirrel
Eastern Fox Squirrel
Red Squirrel
Southern Flying Squirrel
Northern Flying Squirrel

Family Castoridae
Beaver

Family Cricetidae (Muridae or Arvicolidae)
Marsh Rice Rat
Eastern Harvest Mouse
Deer Mouse
White-footed Mouse
Cotton Mouse
Golden Mouse
Hispid Cotton Rat
Allegheny Woodrat
Meadow Vole
Rock Vole
Woodland Vole
Southern Red-backed Vole
Muskrat
Southern Bog Lemming

Family Muridae
Black Rat
Norway Rat
House Mouse

Family Dipodidae (Zapodidae)
Meadow Jumping Mouse
Woodland Jumping Mouse

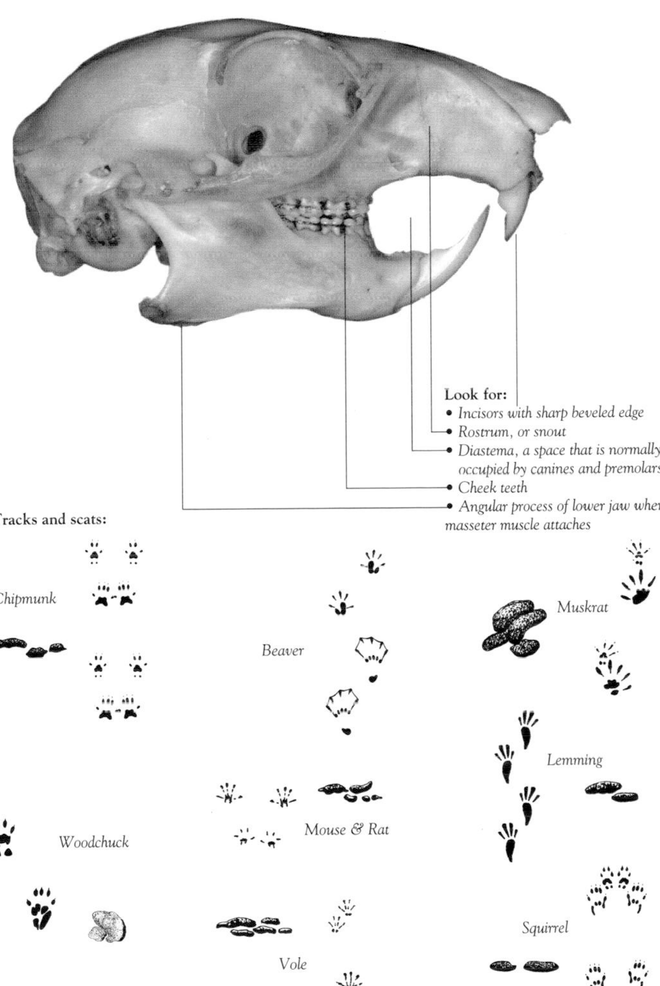
Look for:
• Incisors with sharp beveled edge
• Rostrum, or snout
• Diastema, a space that is normally occupied by canines and premolars
• Cheek teeth
• Angular process of lower jaw where masseter muscle attaches
Tracks and scats:
Chipmunk
Beaver
Muskrat
Lemming
Woodchuck
Mouse & Rat
Squirrel
Vole

EASTERN CHIPMUNK

© Dwight Kuhn

Tamias striatus

7 1/5" - 11 1/5" length
(18.3 - 28.5 cm)

2 4/5 - 5 3/10 oz
(80 - 150 g)

The background color of the chipmunk's head, sides and back of the body are light to dark reddish brown and the underside is white. The rump is rust colored and the shoulders are grayish. The presence of five dark and two white stripes on the body quickly identify this species. Two white stripes are located above and below the eyes. The dorsal surface of the tail is blackish brown and the tail is flat. The ears stand out prominently and are rounded.

◆ **STATUS & HABITAT**—This chipmunk can be found in a variety of deciduous and mixed forests. It frequents the forest edges, rock piles, brushy areas, and areas with an abundance of fallen logs. It is a very significant mammal in the park.

The eastern chipmunk is the only chipmunk found in the East. In contrast, there are over 20 species of chipmunk in the West. In the Americas, this chipmunk occurs from the Atlantic coast of Canada to western Canada. Its range extends south to Louisiana and northwest South Carolina. This rodent is absent from the southern coastal plain and most of Florida

The Latin genus name, *Tamias*, translates into "storer," an excellent description of its food storage behavior in the fall. Its habit of burying seeds and nuts helps disperse and germinate many species of trees and its burrowing habit aerates and mixes the soil. Two to eight young are born per litter and these young can in turn breed when they are three to 12 months old. Population densities in good habitat may reach 15 per acre. Generally these rodents can live up to one to three years in the wild. They are preyed upon by bobcat, coyote, weasel, mink, foxes, snakes, and birds of prey.

These rodents forage primarily on the ground, seeking nuts, acorns, seeds, buds, berries, roots, fungi, mushrooms, and fruits. They also eat insects, frogs, salamanders, young mice, small snakes, and bird eggs and nestlings.

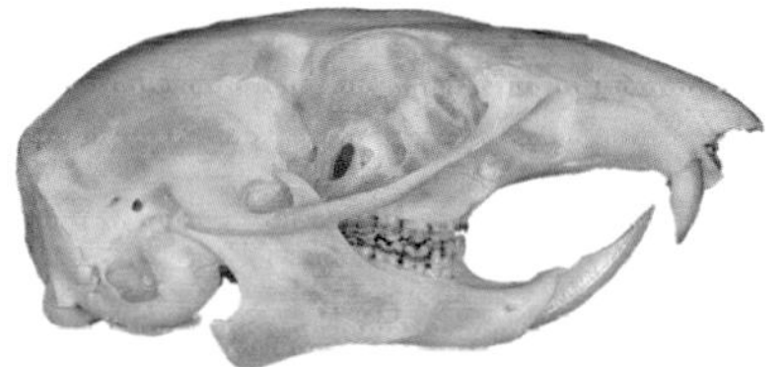

Chipmunks possess internal cheek pouches and they will cram so much food into their mouths that their heads almost triple in size. They cache food in their burrows, under rocks, in hollow logs, or on the surface.

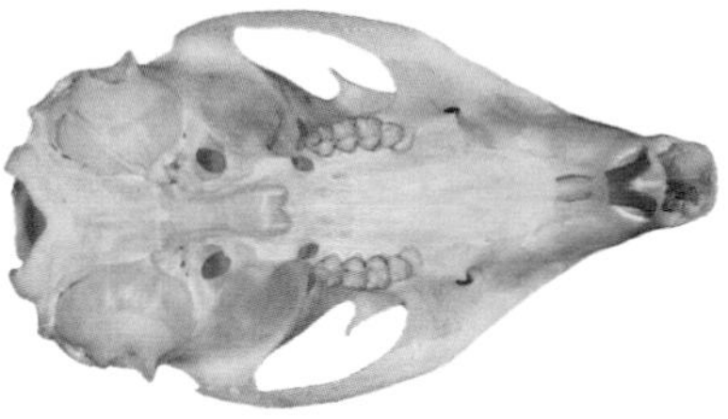

Chipmunks are diurnal

and terrestrial, but they also spend time foraging in trees and use trees to escape from danger. They are very vocal, making a "chuck" or "chip" call as a warning. The chipmunk forms long (up to 30 feet) and complex burrow systems that contain a nest chamber and other chambers used for food caches.

The chipmunk hibernates during winter, attaining a body temperature of 5° C. However, during mild winter weather individuals will forage on the surface.

© Dwight Kuhn

A chipmunk den.

Marmota monax

16 1/2" - 26 2/5" length
(42 - 67 cm)

5 - 13 lbs
(2.3 - 5.9 kg)

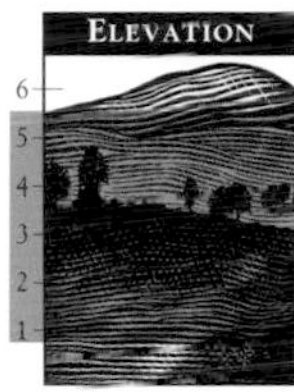

Bill Lea

The background color of the woodchuck's head, sides and back are dark gray to brown and the underside is reddish brown. The dorsal pelt has a grizzled appearance with the intermixing of white and light brown hairs. The feet and legs are short and blackish brown to black. The tail is flattened, short, and black or dark brown. The head is broad and short and the ears are low but stand out and are rounded. The woodchuck, like all squirrels, possesses a postorbital process in its skull that is triangular in shape above each eye socket.

◆ **STATUS & HABITAT**—The woodchuck, groundhog, or whistle-pig is the largest ground squirrel in the deciduous forests of the eastern United States. The woodchuck is the only member of the genus *Marmota* found in the East, in contrast to the five species that reside in the West. In the Americas the woodchuck occurs from the Atlantic coast of Canada westward to the mid sections of western Canada to parts of Alaska. The woodchuck's range then extends from Maine to North Dakota south to Oklahoma and parts of Mississippi to North Carolina and northwest South Carolina. This rodent is absent from Florida and from the coastal plain from Mississippi to North Carolina.

The woodchuck can be found in forest edges bordering fields, near streams located in fields and meadows, along fence rows, and along road right of ways. It is not as abundant as it was prior to the development of the park. The woodchuck is primarily associated with open meadows, farmland, and forest edges. As the cleared land reverted to forests, preferred habitat decreased. Woodchuck burrows serve as refuges for opossums, rabbits, skunks, foxes, snakes, amphibians, and box turtles. Population densities may reach one individual per ten

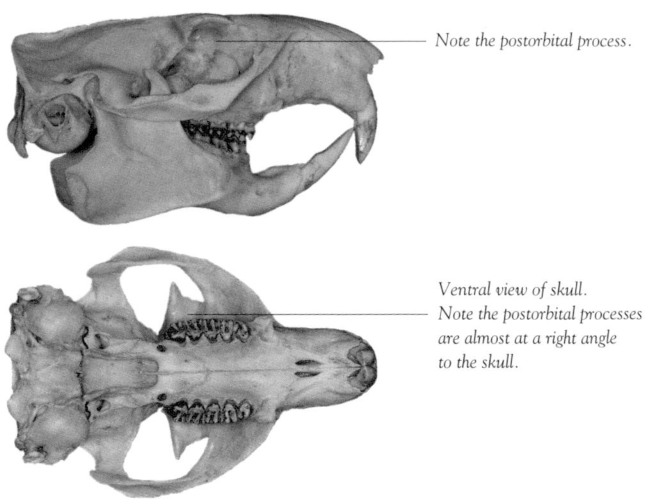

Note the postorbital process.

Ventral view of skull. Note the postorbital processes are almost at a right angle to the skull.

Bill Lea

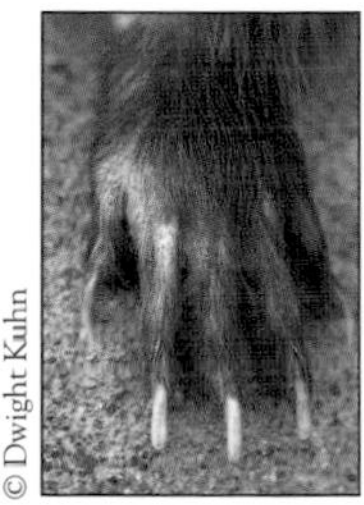

© Dwight Kuhn

acres. Generally these rodents live two to six years in the wild.

Woodchucks forage primarily on the ground, seeking herbaceous vegetation such as clover, dandelion, stonecrop, grasses, vegetable crops, blackberries, and other fruit. They will also consume bark and the buds of trees and shrubs. They are prey for coyote, bear, foxes, and birds of prey.

Woodchucks can climb trees to escape from danger. If alarmed, an individual will stand upright on its hind legs next to its burrow entrance and utter a sharp whistle. The woodchuck forms extensive and complex burrow systems that contain several nest chambers and chambers for fecal and urine deposition. The main burrow entrance always has a pile of excavated dirt around it.

Woodchucks fatten during the fall and hibernate during the winter, attaining body temperatures as low as 3 - 5° C.

Eastern Gray Squirrel

© Dwight Kuhn

Sciurus carolinensis

15″ - 21 7/10″ length
(38.3 - 55 cm)

10 1/2 - 26 1/2 oz
(300 - 750 g)

The gray squirrel is so named because of its general body color. It is a medium-sized tree squirrel with a brownish gray color to the head, sides and back of the body. The mid-dorsal area is slightly brown. The eyes are surrounded by a whitish ring and the back of the ears are white. The underparts are usually white to grayish white. The tail is bushy and the hairs on the tail are banded tan, black, and white. The skull of the gray squirrel has five upper cheek teeth on each side unlike the fox squirrel which possesses four upper cheek teeth on each side. It is also known as the cat squirrel because of one of its cat-like calls.

Gray squirrel's nest.

◆ STATUS & HABITAT—The gray squirrel is commonly seen throughout the park. Ideal habitat consists of mature oak, hickory, and beech trees with tree cavities. They also tend to be abundant along river bluffs and wooded river bottoms. It is one of the most abundant mammals in the East in both deciduous and mixed forests. In the Americas this squirrel occurs from parts of Maine to southwestern Saskatchewan and extends south from North Dakota to Texas and east to the Atlantic coast.

This squirrel out-competes the fox squirrel in closed-canopy forests. Generally they can live up to 12 years in the wild. They are prey for bobcat, coyote, raccoon, foxes, snakes, and birds of prey.

These squirrels forage in the trees and on the ground seeking beechnuts, hickory nuts, acorns, and conifer seeds. They will also eat buds, flowers, bulbs, tubers, twigs, bark, berries, mushrooms, fungi, fruits, and insects. They occasionally eat bird eggs and nestlings. These squirrels hoard food by burying nuts in the soil or leaf litter. They are beneficial in the dispersal and germination of a variety of trees. Research has shown that an individual can recover over 85% of the buried nuts using its keen sense of smell.

Gray squirrels are diurnal and very much at home in the trees. They can leap up to 15 feet from branch to branch. They tend to stay within close proximity of trees and rarely venture far into open areas.

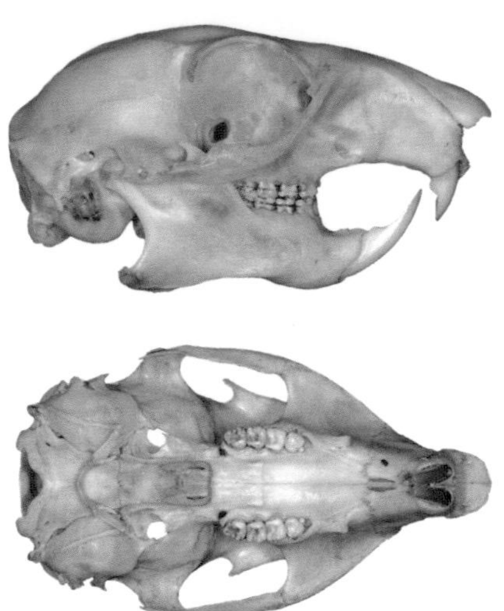

This species has been known to make major movements (emigrations) from an area when population pressures increase or the nut crop fails. They are very vocal, making barking and chattering sounds with vigorous movement of their tails. They build nests in natural tree cavities in mature trees as well as in the branches of large trees. Their nest may be up to the size of a bushel basket and up to eight squirrels may share a winter nest.

Eastern Fox Squirrel

Rolf Nussbaumer

Sciurus niger

17 9/10" - 27 1/2" length
(45.4 - 69.8 cm)

17 3/5 - 52 9/10 oz
(500 - 1500 g)

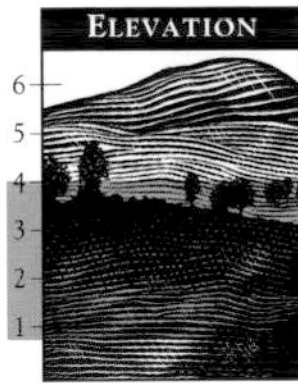

The fox squirrel is so named because its tail "resembles" the tail of the red fox. It is a large squirrel with a squarish profile to the head. In the Southeast, the head, sides, and back of the body can be black, pale gray, or rusty brown. The top of the head is black and the nose, ears and paws are a creamy white or orange brown. The gray fur looks grizzled because the tips of the hairs are black. The underparts are usually yellowish white with the underside of the tail reddish buff. Some color phases possess ochraceous orange underparts. Many color phases can, at times, be found in one locality. This rodent is unique among mammals in accumulating uroporphyrin in its teeth and bones which gives them a pinkish color.

◆ **STATUS & HABITAT**—The fox squirrel can be found in open and mature stands of pine, oak, hickory and sweetgum. They avoid areas with dense ground cover. Populations of this species have declined throughout the East. The decline in mature pine and hardwood forests is part of the reason for the decline of these squirrels, especially in the Northeast. Fire suppression in pine forests is also cited as a reason for their decline.

This squirrel is the largest tree squirrel in the Western Hemisphere and is also one of the most variable in color. In the Americas this squirrel occurs from parts of New York to North Dakota and extends south to Texas and northeastern Mexico. This species occurs east to South Carolina and the coastal plain region of North Carolina. Ideal

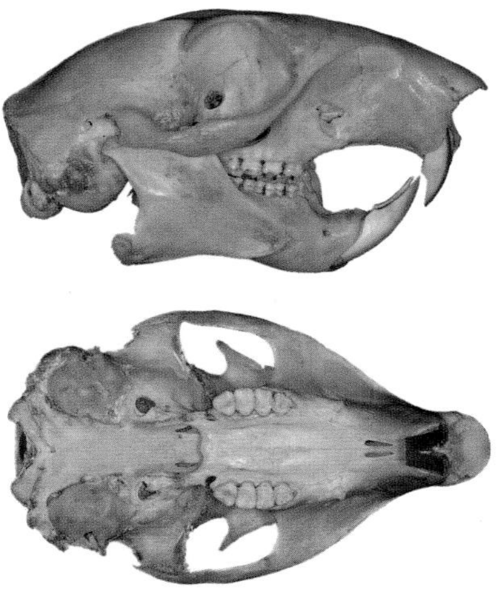

habitat for the fox squirrel is not common in the park. Closed canopy forests are better habitat for gray squirrels and these squirrels outcompete the fox squirrel in such places. Fox squirrels can live six to 12 years in the wild. They are prey for bobcat, coyote, raccoon, foxes, snakes, and birds of prey.

Fox squirrels forage primarily on the ground, seeking beechnuts, hickory nuts, acorns, and conifer seeds. They are beneficial in the dispersal and germination of a variety of tree seeds and nuts. They will also eat buds, bulbs, tubers, twigs, bark, berries, fungi, fruits, and insects. These squirrels hoard food by burying nuts in the soil or leaf litter.

Edward Pivorun

Rolf Nussbaumer

Fox squirrels are not as agile in the trees as gray squirrels and will forage in a field a great distance from the nearest tree. They are very vocal, making barking and chattering sounds. Fox squirrels nest in natural tree cavities in old mature trees as well as in the forks of large trees.

Red Squirrel

© Dwight Kuhn

Tamiasciurus hudsonicus

9 4/5″ - 13 4/5″ length
(25.0 - 35.0 cm)

4 9/10 - 8 4/5 oz
(140 - 250 g)

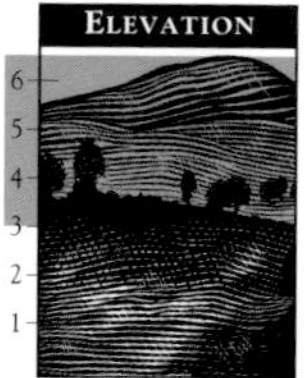

The head, sides, and back of the red squirrel are reddish gray to reddish brown and the underside is white to grayish white. There is a prominent white eye ring. In the summer a black stripe separates the white underside from the reddish upperparts. In the winter a broad rusty red band extends from the head to the tail, the black stripe disappears and black or reddish tufts of hair are prominent on the ears. The winter pelt of this squirrel is brighter than the summer pelt.

◆ **STATUS & HABITAT**—The red squirrel is one of the most common squirrels in coniferous

© Dwight Kuhn

© Dwight Kuhn

and high elevation forests, but it is also found in deciduous and mixed forests. This small squirrel is also known as a mountain boomer, chickaree, pine squirrel, and fairy diddle. In the Americas this squirrel has the largest range of any squirrel, occurring from the Atlantic coast of Canada to Alaska. The red squirrel extends south following the Appalachian Mountains to South Carolina in the East and to Illinois in the Midwest. In the West, the species ranges from Washington to Arizona, following the Rocky Mountains.

The red squirrel may harvest a large proportion of the conifer seeds in a given area and actually influence the natural regeneration of a forest. Conversely, it aids in the dispersal of important fungi that are essential for conifer forest health. Population densities in good habitat may reach 18 to 20 individuals per acre. Generally these rodents can live up to five years in the wild. They are prey for bobcat, coyote, foxes, snakes, and birds of prey.

Red squirrels forage primarily in trees seeking beechnuts, hickory nuts, acorns, conifer seeds, sycamore seeds, buds, berries, twigs, fungi, and fruits. They occasionally eat insects and bird eggs and nestlings. An unusual food item is the dried sap of sugar maple trees. A squirrel will gnaw the bark and will either immediately lick the sap or allow it to dry and return at a later time to lick the more concentrated sap. This species is able to eat many species of "deadly" mushrooms with no apparent ill effects. These squirrels store food in large food caches, or middens, in hollow trees, logs, stumps, or on the surface. Some of these caches are used over many years and more than a bushel of seeds and cones can be stored.

Red squirrels are very vocal, making barking and chattering sounds (hence the nickname "boomer"). They may build nests in woodpecker and natural tree cavities, in the branches of trees, or under rock piles. In very cold weather they will burrow under the snow.

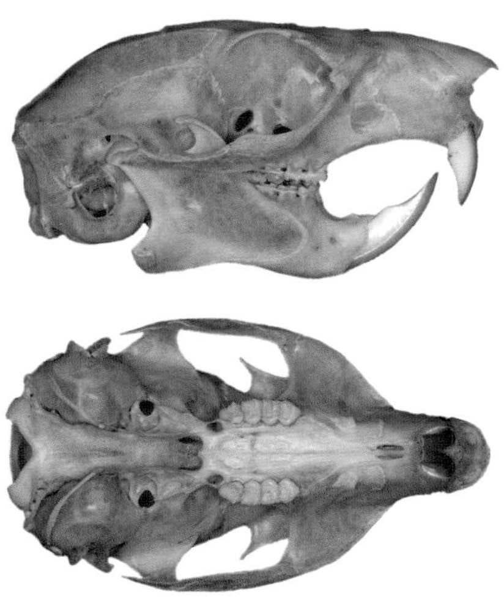

SOUTHERN FLYING SQUIRREL

Glaucomys volans

7 7/10" - 10 2/5" length
(19.6 - 26.5 cm)

1 3/10 - 3 oz
(38 - 87 g)

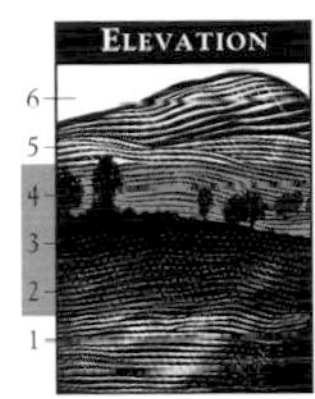

Maslowski Wildlife Productions

The head and back of the southern flying squirrel are buffy brown to gray in color. The underbelly fur is white with each hair white from base to the tip. This is a diagnostic characteristic that aids in identifying a southern versus northern flying squirrel. The fur is extremely dense and soft which helps reduce air friction during gliding. The body appears to be horizontally flattened, another aid for gliding. The primary anatomical adaptations for gliding are the patagia, folds of skin that extend from the wrists to the ankles, and the soft, broad, flat tail. The patagia are unfolded as gliding structures when the animal spreads its front and rear legs. The tail is used as a rudder and stabilizer and these animals can make turns in midair that approach a right angle. The eyes are relatively large and ringed in black.

◆ **STATUS & HABITAT**—The southern flying squirrel is one of the most common rodents in deciduous forests in the South. However, this squirrel is rarely seen since it is entirely nocturnal. In the Americas, the southern flying squirrel occurs from southern Quebec and Nova Scotia to western Minnesota. It ranges south to eastern Texas and Florida and isolated populations are found at high elevations in Mexico and Central America.

The southern flying squirrel prefers mature pine-oak and oak-hickory forest, but it can be found in a variety of deciduous and mixed forests. This species is rarely found in high elevation spruce-fir forests. Population densities are usually between three to five individuals per acre. They are prey for bobcats, weasels, raccoons, foxes, snakes, and birds of prey.

These squirrels forage primarily in the trees for hickory nuts, beech nuts, acorns, and buds. They also seek underground fungi, mushrooms, lichen, seeds, berries, fruits, insects, spiders, slugs, bird eggs, nestlings, and carrion. They are the most carnivorous of any North American squirrel species. In the fall these squirrels cache nuts in their nests,

Edward Pivorun

Bill Beatty

Above: A baby flying squirrel with developing patagia.

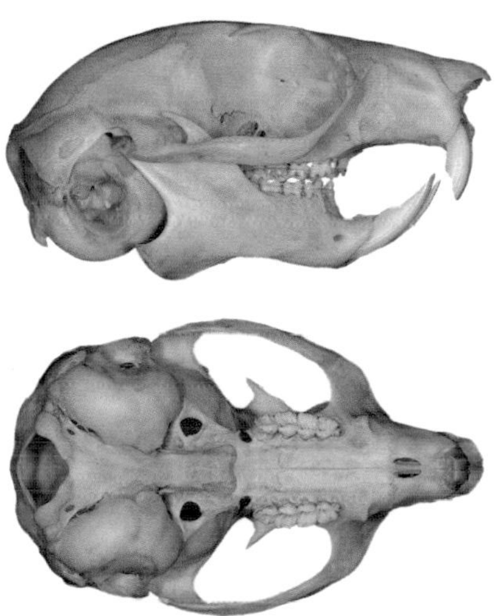

between branches, in tree trunk crevices and cavities, and also underground.

These rodents glide, but do not fly, from tree to tree, covering distances of 20 to 30 feet per glide. Glides of 100 to 200 feet have been documented. They build nests in woodpecker cavities and are considered competitors for nest sites with the endangered red-cockaded woodpecker. This species is more aggressive than the northern flying squirrel and evidence indicates that the southern flying squirrel can displace the northern. Occasionally they construct outside leaf nests or modify bird or gray squirrel nests. Most nests are located 15 to 20 feet above ground. In winter, three to eight individuals may be found co-inhabiting a single nest. At night these squirrels emit distinctive "tssep" calls and chirps.

Carolina Northern Flying Squirrel

© Dwight Kuhn

Glaucomys sabrinus coloratus

Endangered

9 9/10" - 13 1/2" length
(25 - 34.2 cm)

2 1/2 - 4 9/10 oz
(70 - 140 g)

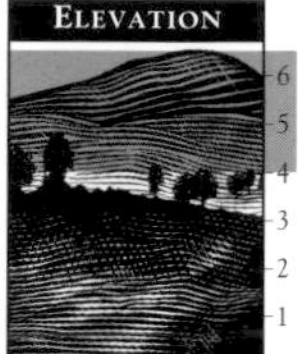

The head and back of the Carolina northern flying squirrel are cinnamon brown to rusty brown in color. The underbelly fur is grayish to buffy gray. This is one diagnostic characteristic that is used to distinguish it from the southern flying squirrel, which has white underparts.

In the northern flying squirrel each hair of the belly region has a grayish base and a white tip. The fur is extremely dense and soft which helps reduce air friction during gliding. The body appears to be horizontally flattened, another aid for gliding. The primary anatomical adaptations for gliding are the patagia, folds of skin that extend from the wrists to the ankles, and the soft, broad, flat tail. A styliform process extends from each wrist to support the front part of the patagia. The patagia are unfolded as gliding structures when the animal spreads its front and rear legs. The tail is used as a rudder and stabilizer and these animals can make turns in midair that approach a right angle. Glides of over 250 feet have been recorded. The eyes are relatively large and ringed in black.

◆ **STATUS & HABITAT**—The Carolina northern flying squirrel is an endangered animal found in the high altitude conifer forests of east Tennessee and western North Carolina. This subspecies is almost never seen since it is rare and entirely nocturnal. Other subspecies of northern flying squirrel are generally common from eastern Alaska throughout most of the forests of Canada. They range south to California and in the Rocky Mountains to Utah and south from Maine to Pennsylvania and west from Michigan to North Dakota. In the Southern states there is also a relict population restricted to the mountains of Virginia and West Virginia, G. *sabrinus fuscus*.

The Carolina northern flying squirrel population size is small and distribution

© Dwight Kuhn

is spotty. The fact that this subspecies is endangered in its southern range and that it occurs in the Smokies makes the park an important haven for this squirrel. Unfortunately, the balsam woolly adelgid has killed many of the Fraser fir trees in the park and the demise of these forests could harm the southern populations. This species is considered an important factor in the dispersal of fungal spores that germinate to form symbiotic fungi that helps maintain forest health. Two to four young are born per litter and up to two litters are produced per year. Population densities are usually between three to four per acre. They can be prey for bobcats, weasels, coyote, foxes, snakes, and birds of prey.

These squirrels forage in the trees and on the ground seeking nuts, underground fungi, mushrooms, lichens, seeds, berries, fruits, insects, bird eggs and nestlings, and carrion.

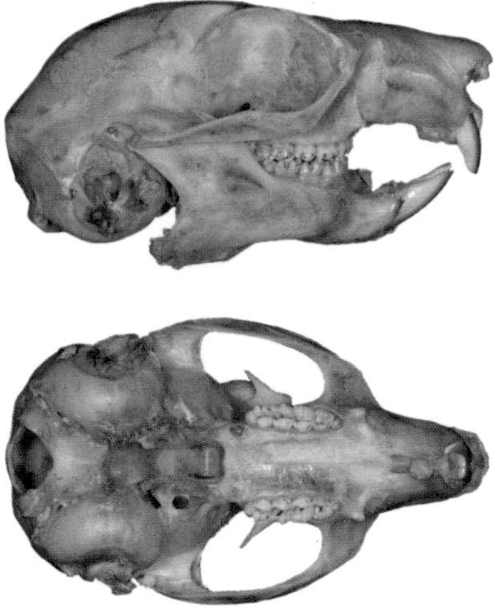

Maslowski Wildlife Productions

Castor canadensis

35 2/5″ - 47 1/5″ length
(90.0 - 120.0 cm)

28 3/10 - 66 lbs
(13 - 30 kg)

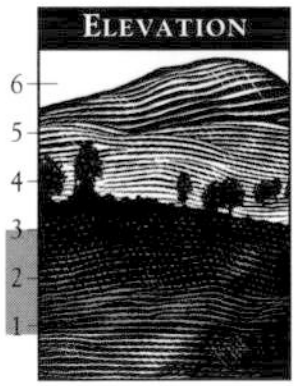

The beaver is the largest rodent in North America and is the only rodent with a large, flat, paddle-like tail. The fur is reddish to blackish brown from top to bottom. The underfur is dense, soft, waterproof and sheds water readily. Aquatic adaptations include transparent nictitating membranes that protect the eyes underwater, the ability to close the nose and ears while underwater, and lips that close behind the teeth to allow transport of food. The large hind feet are partly webbed. Beavers have large yellow upper incisors that are exceptionally strong because of the iron present in the enamel.

Tom & Pat Leeson

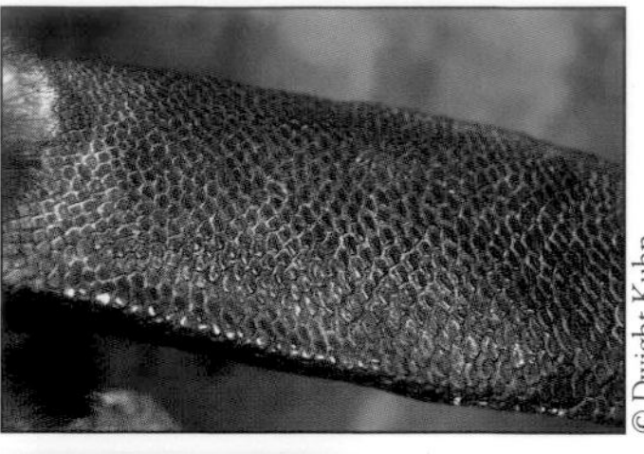

© Dwight Kuhn

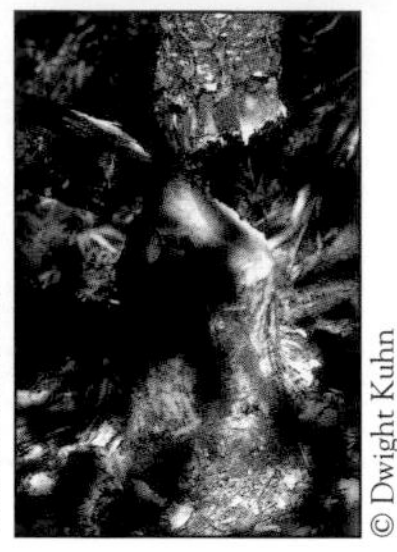

© Dwight Kuhn

The beaver uses its flat tail (above) for propulsion. At left, trees are felled to get at the inner bark.

◆ **STATUS & HABITAT**—This species was probably a significant component of the mammalian communities associated with streams and rivers of the Smokies in former times. The first recent evidence of beavers in the park was in 1966 when beaver dams were discovered in the Eagle Creek area. Most early evidence for beavers in the park was on the North Carolina side. In the last 20 years beaver sign has been observed on the Tennessee side as well. The beaver's return to the Smokies followed reintroductions by state agencies in Tennessee and North Carolina. The steepness of the terrain is the limiting factor regarding the expansion of the beaver's range in the park. If the current flow is too fast, the animals cannot build dams.

Beavers eat the inner bark, twigs and buds of trees such as sweetgum, tuliptree, dogwood, beech, maples, willow, alder, apple, birch, and silverbell. In summer they also eat aquatic succulents, pond lilies, grasses, sedges, duckweed, algae, and rootstock.

Young beavers are preyed upon by bobcats, foxes, and coyotes. Usually one to nine young are born per litter and these young in turn breed when they are two to three years old. These rodents live up to 20 years.

Beavers are more active during night than day. Although known for the lodges they build, individuals that live in rivers construct nests in bank dens that have submerged entrances. Beavers fall and girdle trees to obtain the inner bark. Beavers mate for life. They live in colonies which usually consist of the mated pair, the newborns, and yearlings. They can remain underwater for 15 minutes, but usually only remain submerged for one or two minutes. Their rear feet and tail are used for propulsion and the tail is also slapped across the surface of water as an alarm signal. Trapped air in the fur makes the animal relatively buoyant and provides important insulation against cold water.

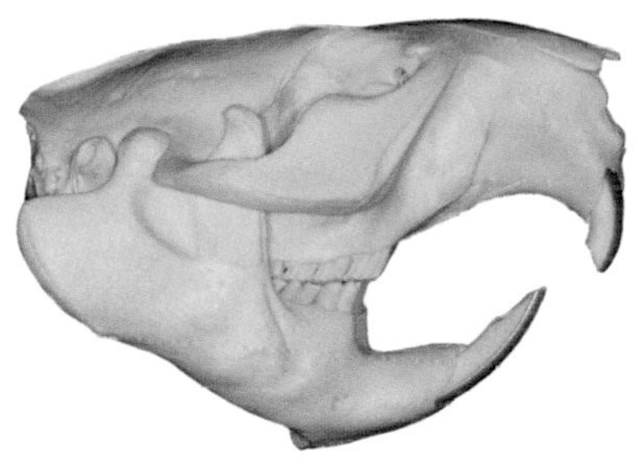

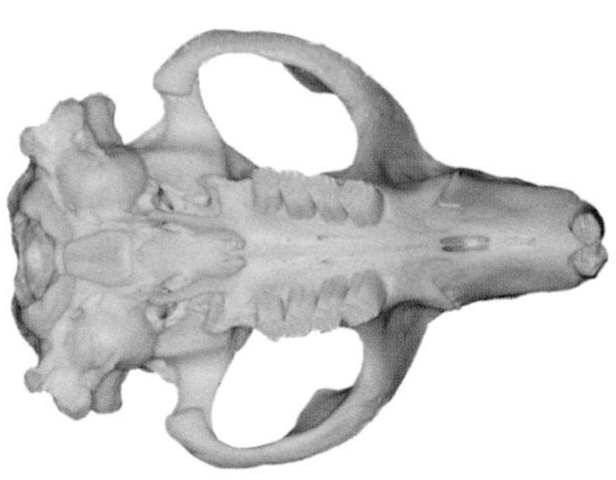

Marsh Rice Rat

Richard K. LaVal/Mammal Image Library, ASM

Oryzomys palustris

7 ½″ - 11 4/5″ length
(19.1 - 30.0 cm)

1 2/5 - 3 oz
(40.0 - 85.0 g)

The marsh rice rat's head, sides, and back are brownish gray and the underside is grayish white. There is a darker brown mid-dorsal stripe. The fur is wooly, smooth, and highly water repellent. The tail is slender, as long as the head and body length, and sparsely haired. The tail is usually not strongly bi-colored but is paler below. The feet are white-gray and the toes of the hind feet are joined by webbing at their base. The ears are relatively small and partly hidden by the fur on the head. This species can be confused with the Norway rat. One diagnostic characteristic is the sparsely haired tail of the marsh rat, in contrast to the naked tail of the Norway rat.

◆ **STATUS & HABITAT**—The marsh rice rat is one of the rodents preferentially found in wet meadows and marshy areas of the South. It inhabits salt marshes on the coast to marshy edges of lakes and streams. At times, this species has been found in upland grasslands with a dense ground cover of grasses and sedges. This species is conspicuously absent from most of the Smokies. Only one specimen has been collected in the park. In the Americas the marsh rice rat occurs from New Jersey to Florida and west to Kansas and southeastern Texas. Its range extends south to Panama.

Generally this species is not associated with mountains. Since the park is primarily forested land, suitable habitat and avenues for dispersal are limited. One to six young are born per litter and these young can in turn breed when they are two months old. In parts of their range five to eight litters are produced per year. In ideal habitats population densities are 10 - 20 individuals per acre. Generally these rodents live less than a year in the wild. They are prey for weasels, mink, raccoon, skunks, foxes, snakes, and birds of prey.

This species is also the primary host for the Bayou virus variant of the hantavirus that causes Hantaviral Pulmonary Syndrome. Humans can contract the disease by breathing in the dry urinary and fecal products stirred up with dirt.

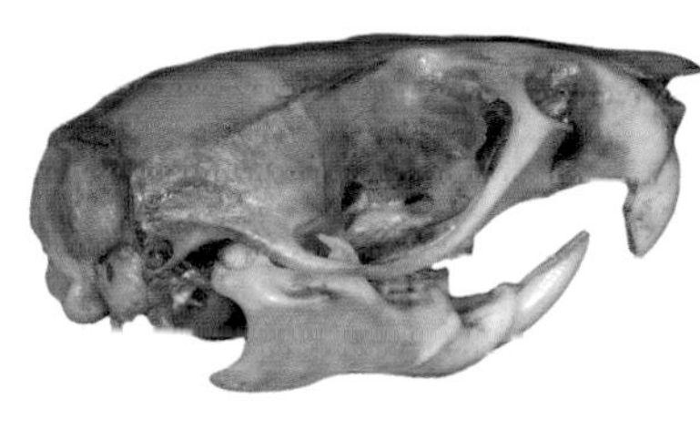

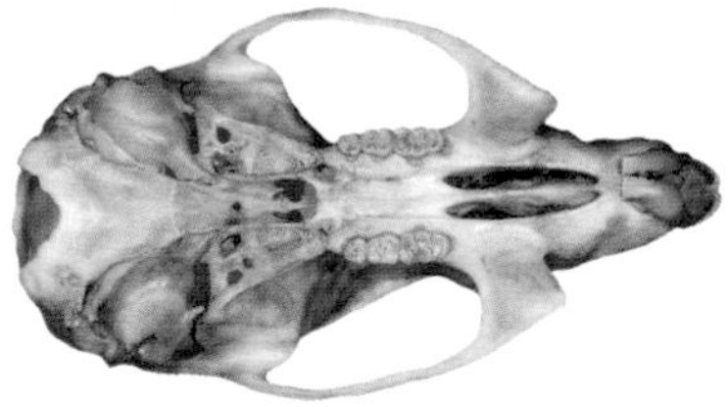

Marsh rice rats eat grasses and sedges, green vegetation, fruits, berries, and nuts. However, this species is considered a highly carnivorous rodent feeding on carrion, fish, baby turtles, birds, bird eggs, crabs, snails, and insects.

Unlike the majority of small rodents, this species is an excellent swimmer and dives of up to 30 feet (10 m) have been recorded.

Eastern Harvest Mouse

James F. Parnell

Reithrodontomys humulis

3 3/10" - 6" length
(10 - 15.2 cm)

1/5 - 1/2 oz
(5.8 - 15 g)

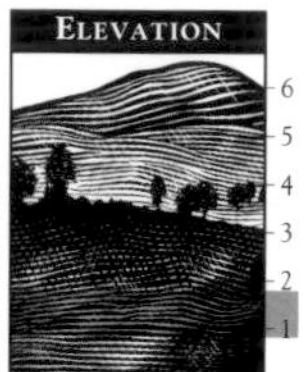

The head, sides, and back of the eastern harvest mouse's body are brownish gray and the underside is grayish white. The middle section of the back is darker brown. The tail is slender, shorter than the head and body length, sparsely haired and bi-colored, brown above and grayish white below. The feet are gray or white. This mouse is the smallest rodent in the park and one of the smallest rodents in the world. It can be confused with the deer mouse, white-footed mouse, and the house mouse. One diagnostic characteristic is the grooves on the front surfaces of the upper incisors.

◆ **STATUS & HABITAT**—The eastern harvest mouse is one of the rodents found in grassy fields, in briar patches and wet meadows in the South. However, this species is conspicuously absent from most of the park. Fewer than ten specimens have been collected in the Smokies. In the Americas, the harvest mouse occurs from Maryland to Florida and west to Arkansas and southeastern Texas.

Generally this species is not associated with mountains. Since the park is primarily forested land, suitable habitat and avenues for dispersal are limited. However, the grasslands of Cades Cove are suitable and extensive habitat for the harvest mouse. These animals have been observed in many localities adjacent to the park. They are usually uncommon and high population densities are rare. Generally they live six months to a year in the wild. They are prey for weasels, foxes, snakes, and birds of prey.

Seeds of grasses and herbs are the primary foods for this species. However, green vegetation and insects are also consumed. Eastern harvest mice store seed in the fall for food over the winter months.

These rodents are active at night. There is evidence they do not occupy fields that harbor the hispid cotton rat. Little is known about their population dynamics since they are very difficult to trap. These mice are excellent climbers and feed above ground in tall grasses and weeds. Nests are globular, made of grass, and are located in thick clumps of grass, in vines or tall weeds. Some nests may be in burrows or beneath logs or rocks.

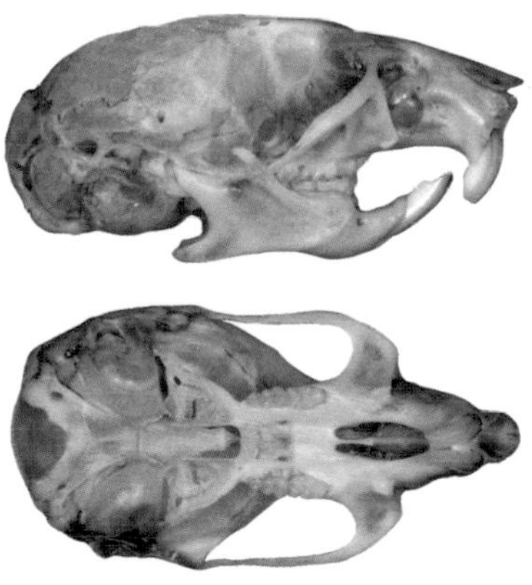

Deer Mouse

Edward Pivorun

Peromyscus maniculatus

6″ - 7 3/4″ length
(15.2 - 20.1 cm)

3/8 - 1 1/4 oz
(11 - 35.4 g)

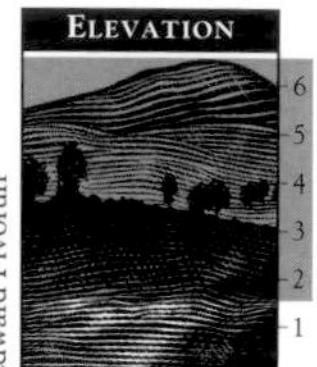

The deer mouse's sides and back are brownish gray with a slightly darker mid-dorsal stripe on the back. The underside and the feet are white (somewhat like a deer). The tail is sharply bi-colored, dark brownish gray above and white with a tuft of longer hairs at the tip. The tail is as long or longer than the head and body. The bi-colored and long tail (2 7/8 - 4 1/2″; 7.3 - 11.3 cm) is an important diagnostic characteristic that distinguishes the deer mouse from both the white-footed and the cotton mouse.

◆ **STATUS & HABITAT**—The deer mouse is the most common rodent in the park and can be found in virtually all habitats. They are less common in grassy fields and dry forests. This species is considered the most widespread and ecologically adaptable of native mice. In the Americas the deer mouse occurs from southeastern Alaska, throughout much of Canada and the U.S. with the exception of most of the Southeast. In North Carolina, South Carolina, and Georgia this species is restricted to the mountain regions and, in the park, it is most abundant at higher altitudes, in cool, moist forests.

These mice show a preference for areas near streams with plenty of rhododendron thickets. They favor forest habitats with an understory of bushes, with fallen and decomposing logs and branches, and stream habitats with undercut banks and exposed roots.

They eat seeds, nuts, flowers, berries, fungi, and fruits. Insects, other invertebrates, and occasionally small birds and mice may also be taken. They hoard seeds in caches located in trees, hollow logs, and underground cavities.

The deer mouse is one of the main prey species for bobcats, weasels, foxes, snakes, and birds of prey. As many as 15 or more mice can be found per acre. Deer mice can breed when they are five to seven weeks old. Up to three to four litters are produced per year. Generally these mice only live one to two years in the wild.

Deer mice are nocturnal. They are adept at climbing trees, bushes, and vines. During food shortages and during cold weather, deer mice enter daily torpor or deep sleep with body temperatures as low as 54° F (12° C) for up to 12 hours.

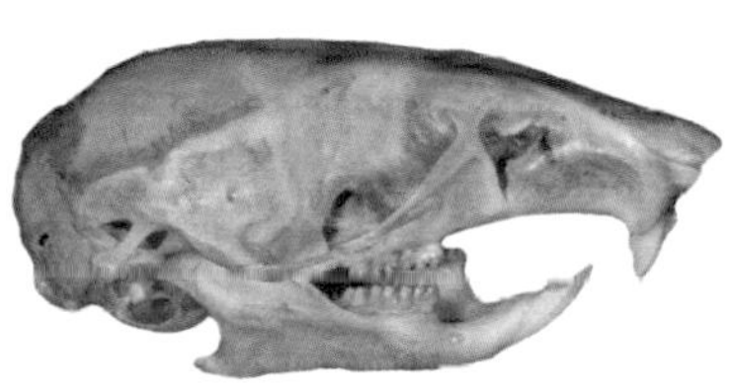

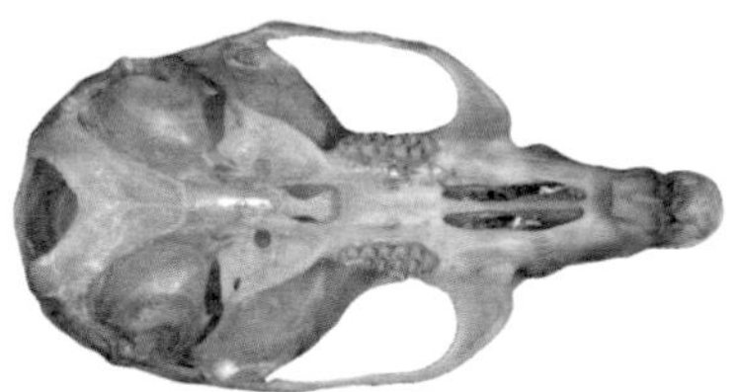

This species is also the primary host for the Monongahela and Sin Nombre variants of the hantavirus that causes Hantaviral Pulmonary Syndrome. Humans can contract the disease by breathing in the dry urinary and fecal products stirred up with dirt in cabins and camping shelters.

WHITE-FOOTED MOUSE

© Dwight Kuhn

Peromyscus leucopus

5 1/2″ - 8″ length
(14 - 20.5 cm)

1/2 - 1 oz
(14 - 28 g)

The sides and back of the white-footed mouse are brownish to dull orange-brown with a slightly darker mid-dorsal stripe on the back. The underside and the feet are white. The tail is indistinctly bi-colored, dark brownish gray above and grayish white below. No tuft of longer hairs is found at the tip. The tail is usually less than 45% of the combined length of the head and body. The presence of a short tail with a dark underside distinguishes the white-footed mouse from the deer mouse.

© Dwight Kuhn

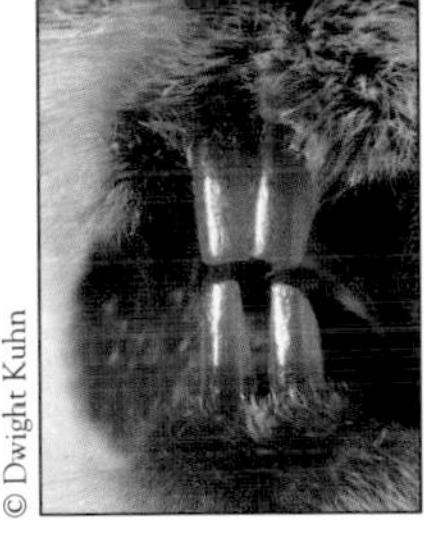

© Dwight Kuhn

◆ **STATUS & HABITAT**—The white-footed mouse is not as common as the deer mouse in the park. However, it is easily confused with the deer mouse and can be found in the same areas.

White-footed mice inhabit deciduous, mixed forests, and occasionally coniferous forests. They show a preference for warm dry forests at low to mid-elevations. They are found in hedgerows, near fallen trees, and in brushy areas adjacent to fields. They will nest in buildings that are close to the edge of woodlands.

White-footed mice eat seeds, nuts, flowers, buds, berries, insects, fungi, and fruits. They hoard seeds in caches located in trees, hollow logs, rock crevices, and underground cavities.

In the Americas the white-footed mouse occurs from the Atlantic coast west to Montana and south into Arizona and southern Mexico. This species avoids the coastal plain regions of the Southeast and is not found in Florida.

This mouse is an important prey species for bobcat, weasels, foxes, snakes, and birds of prey. As many as 13 or more mice can be found per acre. It is considered an important species for dispersal of seeds from trees and shrubs. Up to four litters are produced per year. Generally these mice only live four to eight months in the wild.

This species is also the primary host for the New York-1 variant of the hantavirus that causes Hantaviral Pulmonary Syndrome. This is a disease that causes the lungs to fill with fluid and can result in death. Humans can contract the disease by breathing in the dry urinary and fecal products stirred up with dirt in cabins and camping shelters.

White-footed mice are nocturnal, spending daylight hours in nests in the ground, in rockpiles, in logs, or in the trees. Communal nesting occurs with five or more mice sharing a nest. This species is adept at climbing trees, saplings, bushes, vines, and branches. During food shortages and during cold weather, this species enters daily torpor with body temperatures as low as 63° F (17° C).

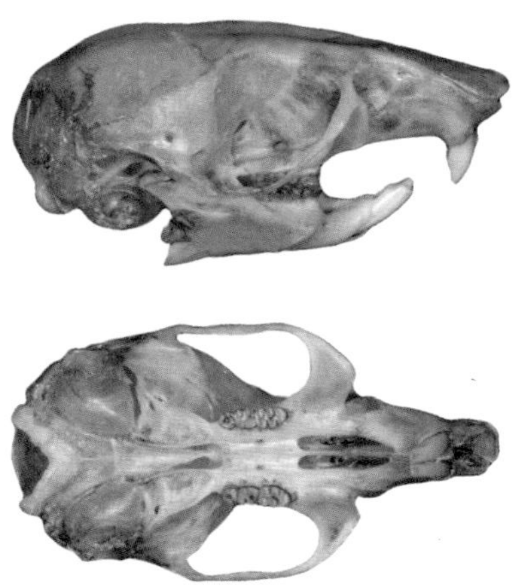

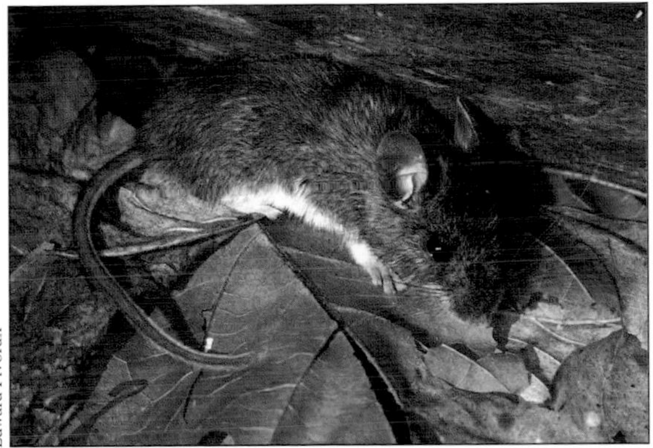
Edward Pivorun

Peromyscus gossypinus
5 1/2″ - 8″ length
(14 - 20.5 cm)

1/2 - 1 oz
(14 - 28 g)

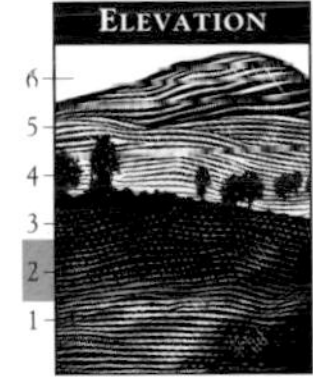

The cotton mouse is larger and heavier than the white-footed and deer mice. The sides and back are chestnut to dark brown with a darker mid-dorsal stripe on the back. The underside and feet are white. The tail is indistinctly bi-colored, dark brown above and grayish white below. No tuft of longer hairs is found at the tip. The tail is usually less than 50% of the combined length of the head and body. The hind foot is 23 - 26 mm long. The darker overall color of the fur and the long hindfeet distinguish the cotton mouse from the white-footed mouse (whose hind feet are less than 23 mm long).

◆ **STATUS & HABITAT**—These mice prefer deciduous forests near streams and rivers. They are found in dense brushy habitats, but can occur in more open habitats. They will enter and nest in buildings that are close to the edge of woodlands.

The cotton mouse is not as common as the deer mouse and white-footed mouse in the park. However, it is easily confused with the white-footed mouse and can be found inhabiting some of the same areas. This species has been found in the northern parts of the park at low to mid elevations. In the Americas the cotton mouse occurs from the Atlantic coast of Virginia and North Carolina to Florida, west to Texas and Oklahoma, and north to southern Illinois and Kentucky.

Cotton mice are prey for bobcats, weasels, foxes, snakes, and birds of prey. Their diet includes seeds, nuts, flowers, buds, berries, fungi and fruits. Adult and larval insects and other invertebrates are also taken.

As many as three or more mice can be found per acre. This species is considered important for dispersal of seeds from trees and shrubs. Usually two to seven young are born per litter and these young can in turn breed when they are seven to ten weeks old. Up to four or five litters are produced per year. Generally these mice only live four to five months in the wild. The entire population of an area is completely replaced on a yearly basis.

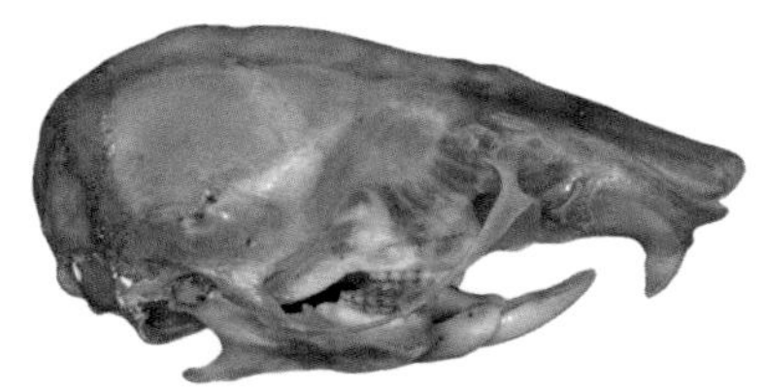

Cotton mice are nocturnal. They spend daylight hours in nests in the ground, in logs, under brush piles, or in the trees. This species is adept at climbing trees, saplings, bushes, vines, and branches.

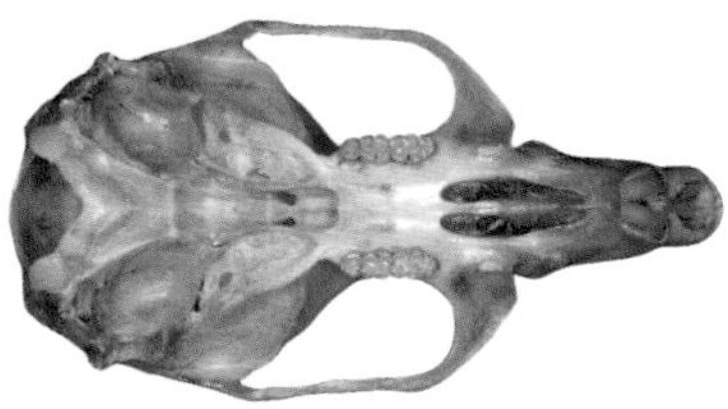

Golden Mouse

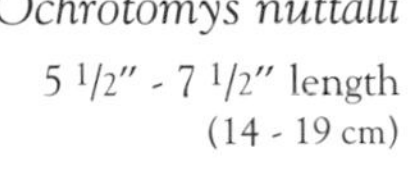

Ochrotomys nuttalli

5 1/2″ - 7 1/2″ length
(14 - 19 cm)

1/2 - 1 oz
(13 - 27 g)

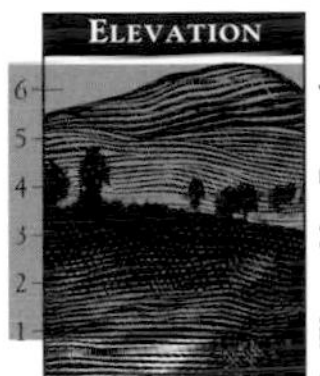

R. Wayne Van Devender

The golden mouse is truly one of the most brilliantly colored and attractive mammals in the park. The golden mouse is rarely seen and most records indicate that this species is primarily found at lower altitudes in the park. However, this species has been observed at Andrews Bald. In the Americas the golden mouse occurs throughout the southeastern region of the U.S. from Virginia to Florida and west to eastern Oklahoma and Texas.

The head, ears, back, and sides of this mouse are covered with a dense and soft fur that is golden to burnt orange in color. The feet and underparts are creamy white with various amounts of ocherous coloration in the belly fur. The tail is short and slightly bi-colored, pale golden brown above and whitish below. This species is relatively unique in that it is semi-arboreal and possesses a semi-prehensile tail that it uses to hang onto branches and vines.

◆ **STATUS & HABITAT**—The semi-arboreal habits of this species make it more difficult for predators to find and capture this mouse.

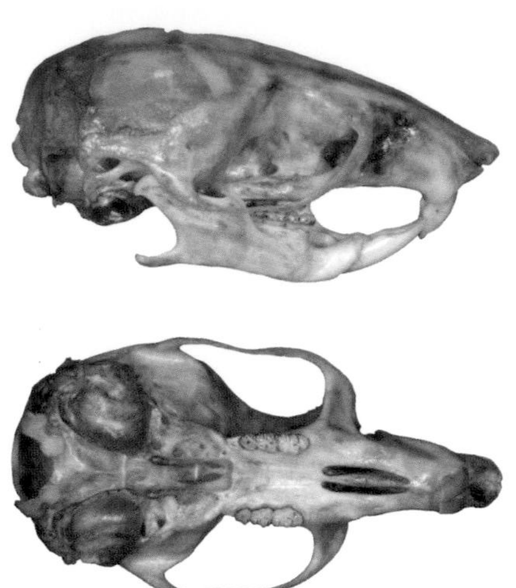

Very little data exists on the predators of golden mice; however, weasels, snakes, and birds of prey probably feed on this species. Population densities are usually relatively low compared to other small rodents in the park with only up to four mice found per acre. Normally one to four young are born per litter and these young can in turn breed when they are two to three months old. Up to two to six litters are produced per year. Generally these mice live six months to two years in the wild.

These mice prefer dense woodlands with a heavy understory of vines, such as greenbrier and grape, and underbrush. They are found in habitats that range from moist deciduous and mixed forests, to boulder-strewn slopes of hemlock forests, to the ridges of mountains. They frequent lowland forested floodplains and the thick brushy areas bordering fields.

Seeds (dogwood, sumac, cherry, and greenbrier), acorns, berries, and insects are consumed. These mice carry their food in cheek pouches and they may consume their food on arboreal feeding platforms located in branches and vines.

This mouse is a nocturnal and highly arboreal species foraging and nesting in thick vegetation and vines. The nests have a single entry hole and are globular, five to eight inches in diameter, and woven from shredded leaves and fibers. Arboreal nests are located from a few inches to over 30 feet above ground. However, nests have been found underground sheltered by logs, rocks, and roots. An individual may have several nests in its home range and the nests can be used for food storage. Up to eight mice have been found sharing a nest. This species also constructs a multitude of flat arboreal feeding platforms throughout its home range.

Hispid Cotton Rat

Edward Pivorun

Sigmodon hispidus

8 3/4" - 14 1/2" length
(22.4 - 36.5 cm)

3 1/2 - 8 1/2 oz
(110 - 245 g)

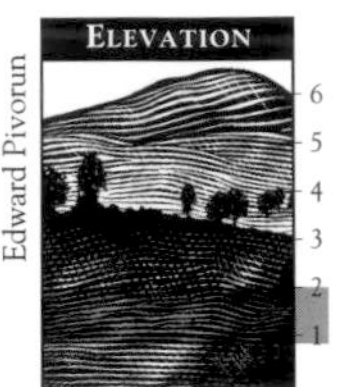

Most of the cotton rat's coat is grizzled; its blackish or dark brownish hairs are interspersed with grayish ones. Its underside is pale to dark gray and its tail is scaly, shorter than the body, and bi-colored. The coloration of its tail is dark brown above and lighter below. The cotton rat's eyes are relatively large and its ears are rounded and partly hidden by the fur on the head.

◆ **STATUS & HABITAT**—Cotton rats prefer more open, agricultural land and thus are not a very significant component of this mostly forested park. However, the grasslands of Cades Cove do provide good habitat. Cotton rats have been observed in many localities adjacent to the park. One to 15 young are born per litter and these young can in turn breed when they are one and a half to two months old. Up to four litters are produced per year. Generally these rodents only live six months in the wild. They are an important prey species for bobcats, weasels, foxes, snakes, and birds of prey.

The cotton rat inhabits old fields dominated by dense grasses, such as broomsedge, weeds, and various forbs. They can be found in grassy roadsides, ditches, and the brushy borders of cultivated and old fields.

Green vegetation is the preferred food, especially leaves and shoots. However, seeds, roots and tubers are also consumed. They occasionally eat insects, crayfish, and the eggs and young of ground nesting birds.

Cotton rats are active day and night. They construct a network of well-defined runways in the dense grasses. This species is also the primary host for the Black Creek Canal virus variant of the hantavirus that causes Hantaviral Pulmonary Syndrome. Humans can contract the disease by breathing in the dry urinary and fecal products stirred up with dirt in cabins and camping shelters.

In the Americas the cotton rat occurs from Virginia to Florida and west to Kansas and New Mexico.

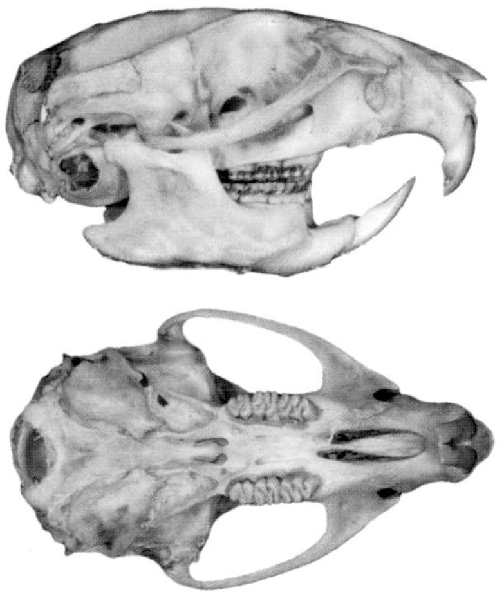

Allegheny Woodrat

Edward Pivorun

Neotoma magister

13 2/5″ - 18 3/10″ length
(34.0 - 46.5 cm)

6 4/5 - 17 1/10 oz
(194 - 485 g)

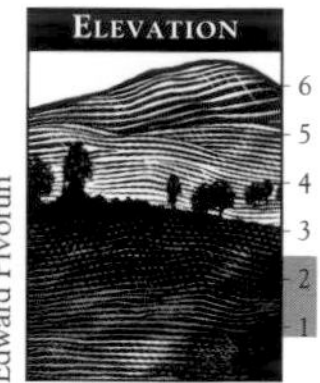

This woodrat is a medium-sized rodent that resembles a large white-footed mouse (*Peromyscus sp.*). The head, sides, and back are brownish gray with black tipped hairs. The underside and the feet are white. The tail is furred and distinctly bi-colored, dark brown above and white below. The ears are prominent and sparsely haired and the vibrissae whiskers are long. The presence of a white underside, long vibrissae, and a furred tail with a white underside distinguish the woodrat from the Norway and black rats.

◆ **STATUS & HABITAT**—The Allegheny woodrat inhabits deciduous forests with rocky outcrops, caves, areas with boulders, and talus and rocky shores of rivers and large streams. It also seeks out old cabins, barns, and outbuildings.

This woodrat ranges from Pennsylvania and New Jersey south to Kentucky, Tennessee, North Carolina and northern Alabama and Georgia. Unfortunately, northern populations are in decline. It is virtually indistinguishable from the eastern woodrat. The Tennessee River acts as a barricade that separates these two species.

The Allegheny woodrat is eaten by predators such as bobcat, weasels, foxes, snakes, and birds of prey. This species has a longer life expectancy compared to other rodents of similar size. Studies have shown that these rats live three to fours years in the wild. Usually one to six young are born per litter and these young usually breed when they are a year old. Up to three litters are produced per year.

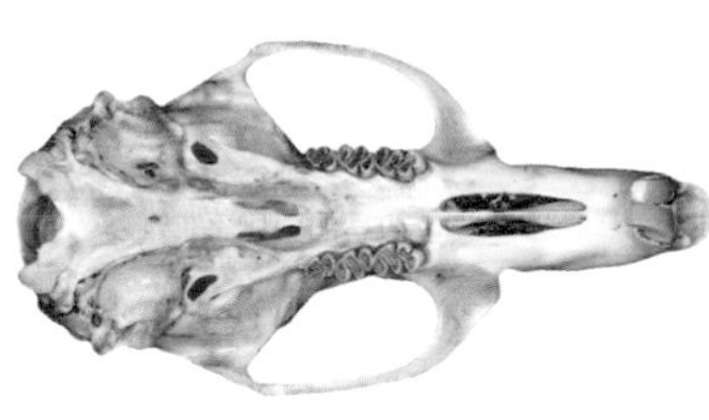

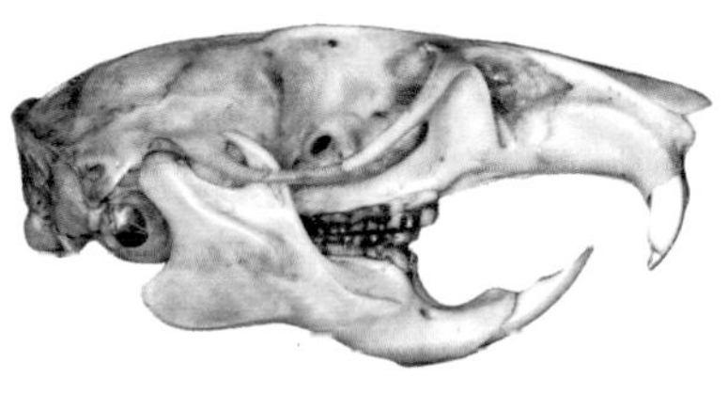

Preferred foods for this woodrat include seeds, nuts, bark, flowers, buds, leaves, stems, tubers, mushrooms, fungi, and fruits. Adult and larval insects are also taken. This species will climb trees and forage for food above ground. Food is stored in the upper sections of their homes in middens, which contain fruit, leaves, nuts, and mushrooms.

The Allegheny woodrat is nocturnal. It spends daylight hours in nests that are found under boulders, in caves, in hollow logs, under stumps, and old buildings. Nests are the size of footballs or larger and are constructed of grasses and shredded bark. Woodrats form latrines outside their nesting areas that consist of a large pile of droppings. They are also famous for creating debris piles that contain food items, sticks, bones, bark, feathers, dung, paper, colored glass, rags, spoons, and other human trash. These debris piles may contain bushels of material. This habit led to these rodents being nicknamed packrats.

MEADOW VOLE

© Dwight Kuhn

Microtus pennsylvanicus

5" - 7 7/10" length
(12.5 - 19.6 cm)

9/10 - 2 1/2 oz
(26 - 70 g)

The meadow vole's body is relatively large and blocky and covered with short, dense fur. The nose and the sides of the body and head are dull chestnut to dark brown in color with black hairs interspersed on the dorsal surface. The underside is silvery gray. The tail is indistinctly bi-colored and about twice the length of the hind foot (longest tail of any vole). The eyes are relatively small and the ears are rounded and partly hidden by the fur on the head. All voles have prismatic dentition, which refers to the cusp pattern on the premolars and molars.

◆ **STATUS & HABITAT**—Meadow voles inhabit moist fields composed of dense grasses and sedges. They may be found in grassy openings in forests and in low moist areas near streams and rivers.

Since the park is primarily forested, suitable habitat and avenues for dispersal are limited. Interestingly, the grasslands of Cades Cove represent suitable and extensive habitat for this vole, but no meadow voles have been captured in this area.

The meadow vole is the main herbivore of open grassy fields in North America. It was first observed in the park in 1965 near the Oconaluftee River. Recently, additional specimens were collected in the park bordering the Cherokee Indian Reservation. This vole has the largest distribution of any rodent in North America. It occurs from the Atlantic coast of Canada to Alaska. It ranges from Maine south to South Carolina and Georgia and west to New Mexico and northeastern Washington. Voles are also called microtine rodents and are related to the lemmings of the arctic regions.

Meadow voles are preyed upon by bobcats, weasels, foxes, raccoons,

snakes, and birds of prey. They exhibit population cycles every three to four years; however, very little data are available for Southern populations. Populations can range from over 150 animals per acre to less than two per acre. Usually one to 11 young are born per litter and these young can in turn breed when they are three weeks old. Up to ten litters are produced per year. Generally these voles only live three to six months in the wild.

These voles eat the seeds and green vegetation of grasses and sedges, rootstock and bark. They store roots, tubers and green vegetation for the winter months.

Meadow voles are active day and night. They are primarily active on the surface using runways in the dense vegetation, but they also form burrows below ground. Their runways are kept well groomed. Piles of droppings (communal toilets) that are greenish brown are deposited in the runways. Nests are globular, made of plant material, and found below ground.

© Dwight Kuhn

© Dwight Kuhn

Above: A meadow vole litter, 24 hours old, in the nest.

Rock Vole

Microtus chrotorrhinus

5 7/10″ - 7 3/10″ length
(14.4 - 18.5 cm)

1 - 1 7/10 oz
(30 - 48 g)

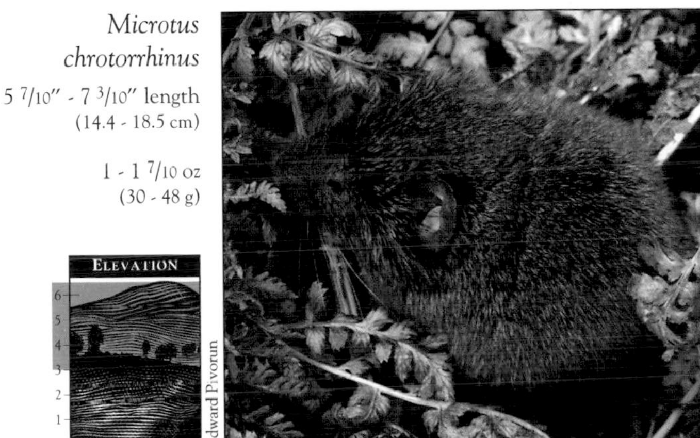

Edward Pivorun

The yellow-orange, saffron, or pale yellow coloration of the snout and rump distinguishes this vole from other eastern voles. The back and sides are blackish brown and the underparts are grayish white. The tail is short and bi-colored, grayish brown above and lighter below. The eyes are relatively small and the ears are rounded and extend beyond the fur on the head. All voles have prismatic dentition, which refers to the cusp pattern on the premolars and molars.

◆ **STATUS & HABITAT**—The rock vole is not one of the more common rodents in the park. This vole is primarily found at higher elevations in moist spruce-fir forests and in areas with moss-covered rocks and logs. They favor habitats with a thick herbaceous layer near streams.

In the Americas the rock vole occurs in the lower southern regions of Canada from the Atlantic coast to northern Minnesota and from northern Maine to northern New York. Populations are then primarily restricted to the Appalachian Mountains from the Virginias to Tennessee and North Carolina. Voles are also called microtine rodents and are related to the lemmings of the arctic.

Rock voles eat roots, fungi (genus *Endogone*), moss, green vegetation, shoots, berries, grasses, and insects. They cut herbaceous vegetation and consume it underground.

Very little information exists on the predators of this species; however, weasels, fox, bobcat, snakes, and birds of prey probably feed on them. Rock voles usually coexist with southern red-backed voles. Population densities can be locally high, but little research has been done on this species. Usually three to four young are born per litter. Age at sexual maturity is not known. Up to three litters are produced per year. Nothing is known about the longevity of these voles in the wild.

Rock voles are nocturnal, as well as diurnal, with some evidence that they are primarily active during the day. Virtually nothing is known about the nests of this species. Rock voles do not climb trees and prefer traveling on the surface and in runways created between and under rocks.

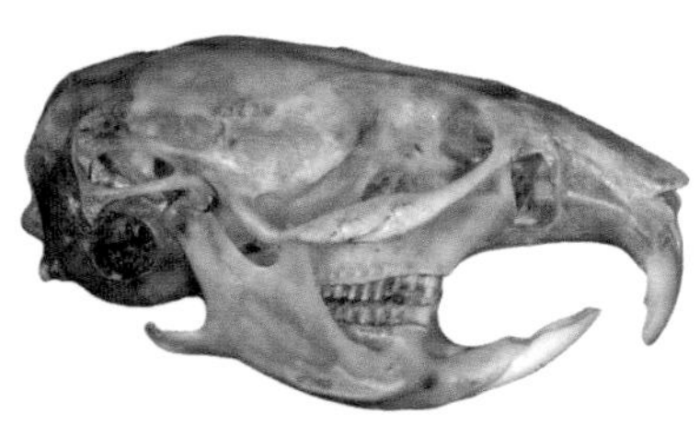

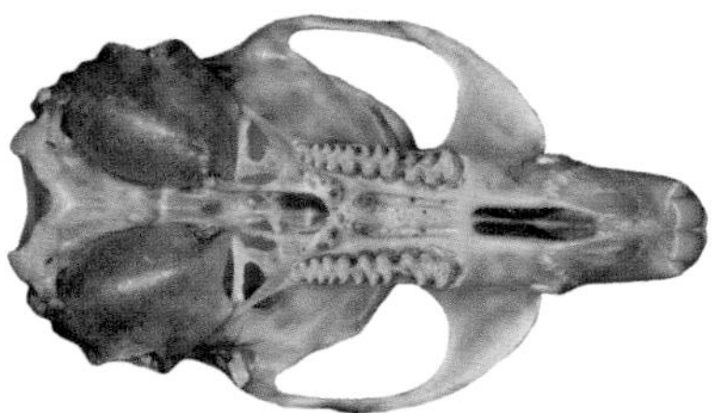

WOODLAND VOLE

Microtus pinetorum

4" - 5 7/10" length
(10 - 14.5 cm)

1/2 - 1 3/10 oz
(14 - 37 g)

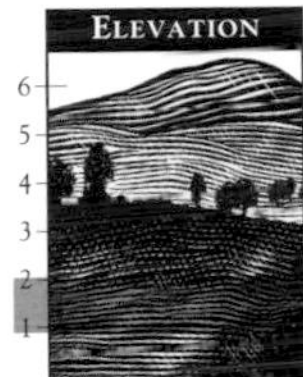

Edward Pivorun

The woodland vole's body is very small and blocky and covered with smooth, short, dense fur that allows for easy passage in its underground burrows. The nose and the sides of the body and head are chestnut brown to cinnamon brown. The underside is silvery gray with buff or chestnut coloration. The tail is indistinctly bi-colored and very short (about the length of the hind foot). The eyes are relatively small and the ears are rounded and nearly hidden by the fur on the head. All voles have prismatic dentition, which refers to the cusp pattern on the premolars and molars.

◆ **STATUS & HABITAT**—The woodland vole is a semifossorial (burrowing) rodent that is rarely seen on the surface. They are extremely hard to capture because of their burrowing habits. They are primarily found at lower to mid elevations in the park. In the Americas the woodland vole occurs from the Atlantic coast west to Iowa and central Texas. These voles are present from southern Ontario to northern Florida. Voles are also called microtine rodents and are related to the lemmings of the arctic regions.

Woodland voles are preyed upon by bobcat, weasels, foxes, opossum, raccoon, snakes, and birds of prey. As many as six voles can be found per acre. This species does not seem to exhibit population cycles in its southern range. Usually one to three young are born per litter and these young can in turn breed when they are two to four months old. Up to five to six litters are produced per year. Generally these voles only live 18 months in the wild.

Woodland voles inhabit deciduous and mixed forests with heavy ground cover and fields bordering woodlands. They show a preference for areas with moist, friable soils that allow for burrowing. They favor habitats with a deep layer of leaf litter.

Their preferred foods include seeds, underground fungi (genus *Endogone*), roots, nuts, tubers, bulbs, fruits, grasses, bark, and plant stems. They store roots and fruits for the winter months.

Woodland voles are nocturnal and diurnal, with short sleep cycles occurring throughout the day and night. They are rarely on the surface. Their nests are located underground in chambers, under logs, or at the base of a tree. These nests are globular, made of plant material, and possess three to four openings. This species is social and more than one female has been found sharing a nest. They construct extensive tunnel systems that are generally three to four inches below the surface. These systems have multiple entrances that are left open.

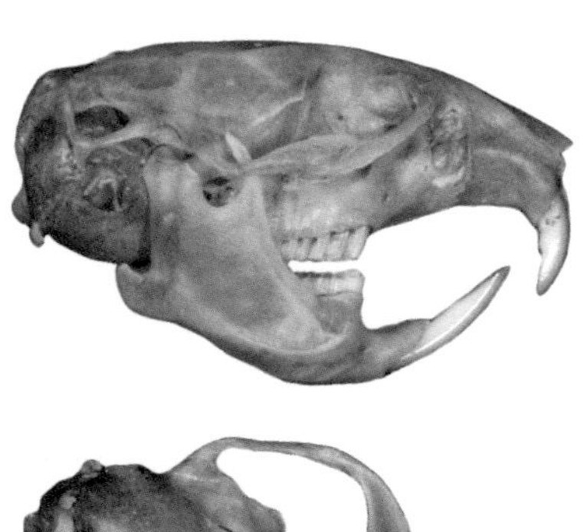

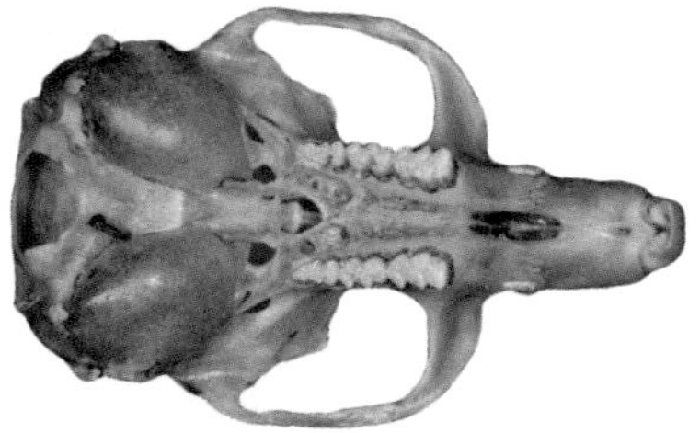

Southern Red-backed Vole

Clethrionomys gapperi

4 7/10" - 6 7/10"
(12.0 - 17.0 cm)

1/2 - 1 1/2 oz
(15 - 42 g)

Edward Pivorun

The southern red-backed vole is mostly gray with a very pronounced broad, reddish mid-dorsal band running from the forehead to the rump. The underside is silvery white to pale yellow. The tail is short and sharply bi-colored, dark brown above and whitish below. The eyes are relatively small and the ears are rounded and extend beyond the fur on the head. The red dorsal band is one diagnostic characteristic that distinguishes this vole from the rock vole that lives in similar habitats.

◆ **STATUS & HABITAT**—The southern red-backed vole is one of the most common rodents at higher elevations in the park and can be found in spruce-fir forests, in beech gaps, and in moist habitats associated with deciduous and mixed forests. They show a preference for areas near streams, bogs, rhododendron thickets, and high elevations. They favor habitats with an understory of bushes, with fallen and decomposing logs and branches, and stream habitats with undercut banks and exposed roots.

In the Americas the southern red-backed vole occurs in the southern tier of Canadian provinces, from Washington to Michigan, in the

Rocky Mountains, and from Maine to the Southeast, with populations restricted to the Appalachian Mountains. Voles are also called microtine rodents and are related to the lemmings of the arctic regions.

This vole is one of the most abundant and dominant prey species for bobcats, weasels, foxes, snakes, and birds of prey. As many as 26 voles can be found per acre. However, population cycles occur at six to ten year intervals and populations may drop to as low as two voles per acre. In turn, these low densities markedly affect predator populations. Usually two to eight young are born per litter and these young can in turn breed when they are two to four months old. Up to two to three litters are produced per year. Generally these voles only live 10 to 20 months in the wild.

Foods favored by red-back voles include seeds, nuts, flowers, berries, fungi, roots, fruits, bark, ferns, lichens, and green vegetation. Underground fungi (genus *Endogone*) are very important food sources in late summer and fall. These voles store shoots, roots, nuts and fungi for the winter months.

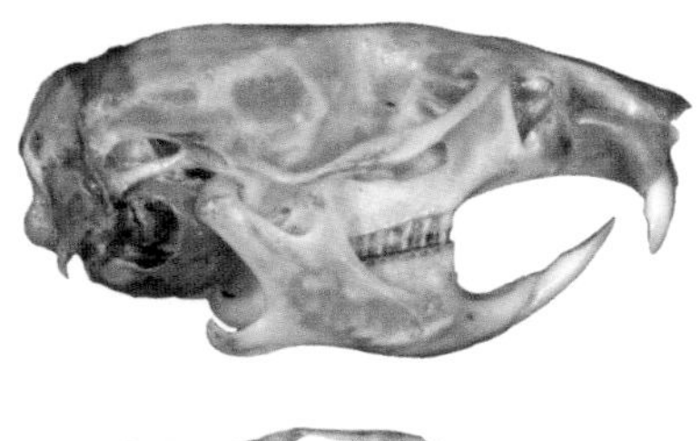

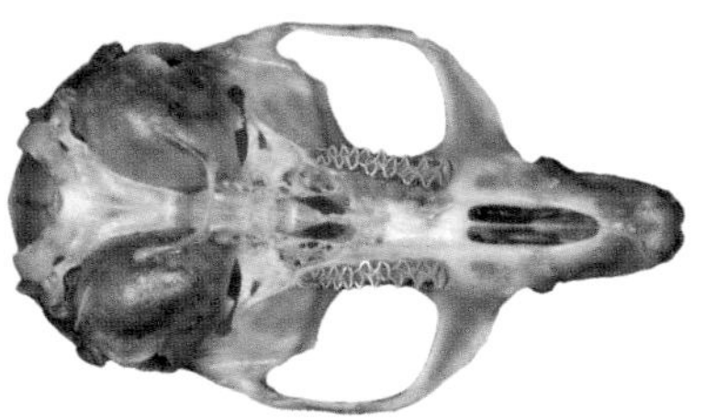

They are active much of the time with short sleep cycles occurring throughout the day and night time. Their nests are globular, made of plant material and moss, and are located underground under rocks, roots, logs or stumps. This species does not climb trees and prefers traveling on the surface, in natural runways created by logs, rocks and tree roots, and in burrows of other mammals.

Ondatra zibethicus

16 1/5" - 28" length
(41 - 71 cm)

24 - 63 1/2 oz
(680 - 1800 g)

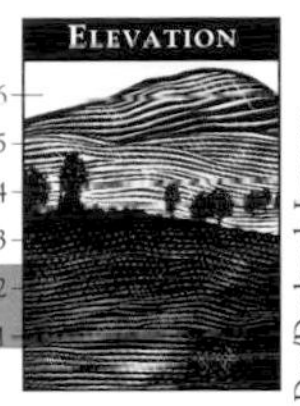

Richard Day/Daybreak Imagery

The muskrat is the largest microtine rodent in the Americas and resembles a giant vole. The fur is chestnut to blackish brown and the underparts are pale gray to cinnamon. The underfur is dense and soft and the guard hairs are long, oily, and reddish brown to black. The fur is relatively waterproof and sheds water readily. The large hind feet are partly webbed and the naked blackish brown tail is laterally compressed. Short stiff hairs on the edges of the hind feet and toes aid in swimming. The ears are rounded and partly hidden by the fur on the head.

The name muskrat refers to the musk glands located near the penis in males. A secretion from these glands is added to the urine and feces. These glands enlarge during the reproductive season and the scent aids in marking territory and in attracting females. All voles have prismatic dentition, which refers to the cusp pattern on the premolars and molars.

Michael Quinton

◆ **STATUS & HABITAT**—This species is a significant component of the mammalian communities associated with streams in the park. Since the park has little standing water, the muskrat is found at lower densities than commonly expected in marshes or lakes. The muskrat occurs from the Atlantic coast of Canada to Alaska. It ranges from Maine south to northeastern South Carolina and Georgia and west to northern California and Washington. This rodent is absent from most of South Carolina, Florida, and Texas, and most of the desert southwest.

Muskrats are preyed upon by mink, bobcats, foxes, raccoons, coyotes, and birds of prey. They exhibit population cycles every ten years; however, very little data are available for Southern populations. Generally these rodents live three to four years in the wild.

Muskrats eat green vegetation and roots of grasses and sedges, some herbaceous plants, and other aquatic plants. They also consume clams, snails, fish, and crustaceans.

The muskrat is a water vole and a microtine rodent related to lemmings. It is active day and night with the greatest activity at night. This rodent can remain underwater for 15 to 20 minutes and can swim submerged for distances of up to 200 feet. The rear feet and the tail are used for propulsion, while the front feet are held against the chest. Trapped air in the fur makes the animal relatively buoyant and provides important insulation against cold water. Although muskrats are known for the lodges they build, individuals that live in rivers construct nests in bank dens that have submerged entrances. Their burrows can be 10 - 50 feet long and are six - eight inches in diameter. They make a saucer-shaped nest of grass at the terminus of the burrow.

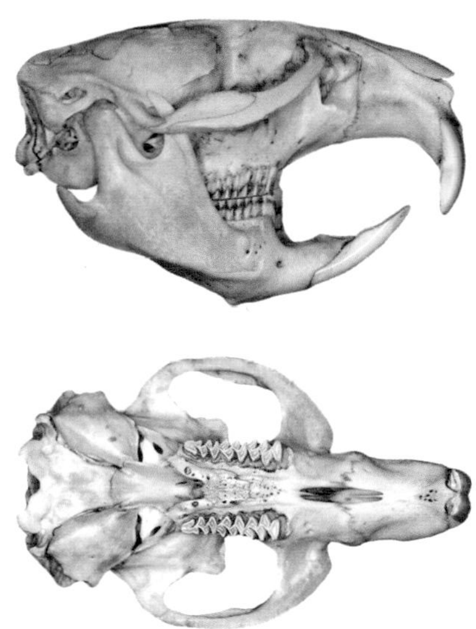

Southern Bog Lemming

R. Wayne Van Devender

Synaptomys cooperi

3 7/10″ - 6″ length
(9.4 - 15.4 cm)

1/2 - 1 4/5 oz
(14 - 50 g)

The southern bog lemming has short feet, a shaggy pelage, a relatively large head, and a short rostrum (snout). The back and sides are grizzled brown with black, brown and gray hairs interspersed and the underparts are grayish white. The brownish black tail is short and weakly bi-colored, blackish brown above and whitish below. The eyes are relatively small and the ears are rounded and do not extend beyond the fur on the head. The tail is very short—equal to or shorter than a rear foot—and the upper incisors have a shallow groove on the front surface.

◆ **STATUS & HABITAT**—The southern bog lemming is not one of the more common rodents in the park and tends to be found in localized populations. This lemming is primarily found at mid to high elevations and can be found in grassy openings in forests, sphagnum bogs, and around moss covered rocks and boulders in moist spruce-fir forests. As long as there is ample forage of grasses and sedges, these microtine rodents seem to maintain viable populations in smaller areas than voles, which compete with them. In the Americas the southern bog lemming occurs in the lowlands of southern Canada from the Atlantic coast to northern Minnesota, Kansas, and Nebraska. Populations extend south from Maine to Virginia and down the Appalachian Mountains to western North Carolina and east Tennessee.

Although these rodents can be locally abundant, they are not widespread and very little research has been done on their distribution in the park. Few individuals have been trapped in the last 50 years. Weasels, foxes, bobcat, snakes, and birds of prey feed on this species. Population densities can be locally high (36 per acre), but normal population densities are two to four per acre. Usually three to four young are born per litter. Age at sexual maturity is two to three months. Up to two to four litters are produced per year. These lemmings live seven to eight months in the wild.

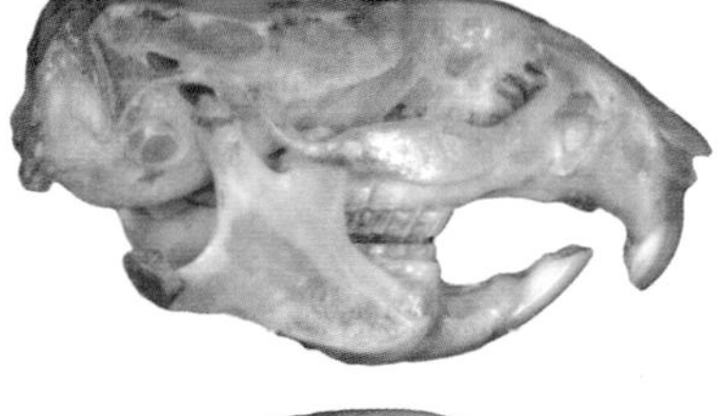

Their diet includes roots, grasses, sedges, fungi (genus *Endogone*), moss, green vegetation, and berries.

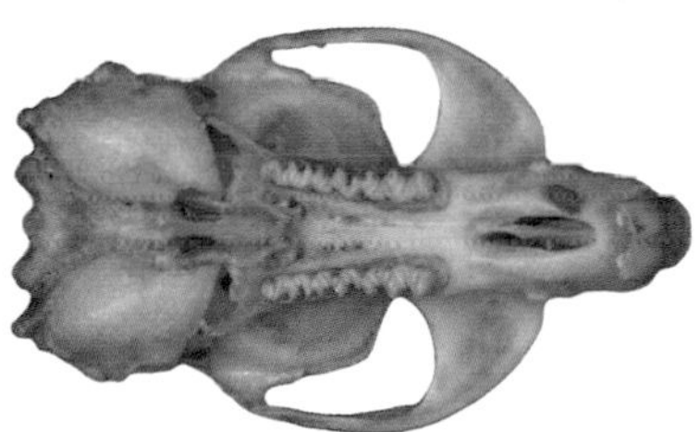

Southern bog lemmings are active most of the day, but especially in the early evening and morning hours. Their nests are balls of grass and leaves three to six inches in diameter, usually underground or concealed in thick vegetation. This species does not climb trees and prefers traveling on surface runways and in runways created underground. Indicators of the presence of this lemming are grass clippings in the runways and fecal droppings that are bright green to yellow in color.

Black Rat

R. Wayne Van Devender

Rattus rattus

Non-native

12 4/5″ - 16 9/10″ length
(32.5 - 43 cm)

5 - 10 oz
(140 - 280 g)

The back and the sides of the black rat's body and head are blackish brown or gray and the underside is dark gray or grayish white. The tail is scaly and slightly longer than the head and body length. The nose is relatively short. The Norway rat has a shorter tail and a lighter body color. These Old World rats possess three rows of cusps on their upper molar teeth, which differs from the two rows observed in the native rats and mice.

◆ **STATUS & HABITAT**—The black or roof rat is one of the most common rodents associated with human habitation in the South. It primarily inhabits buildings and garbage dumps. However, feral populations of these rats will occupy forest stands. This species is absent from most of the park with the possible exception of park buildings. It had been more common in some localities in the park because of past human habitation and agricultural activities. This rat is not native to the Americas and was introduced in the 1500s. In the Americas the black rat occurs from the coastal states of New England to British Columbia and throughout Mexico. The species is especially abundant in the southeastern United States.

Black rat litters range in size from two to 12 young and these young can in turn breed when they are two to three months old. Up to six litters are produced per year. Generally these rodents live only a year in the wild. They are prey for snakes, foxes, and birds of prey. Studies have shown that the Norway rat may occasionally kill and eat black rats. Virtually anything edible is eaten by black rats, with preference given to grain, seeds, and nuts.

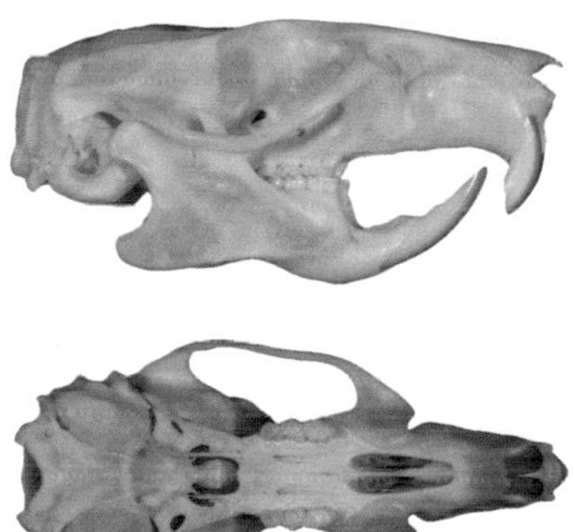

This species is one of the rats associated with the Black Plague in Europe. In the Americas typhus fever can be carried by this rodent.

This species is a more agile climber than the Norway rat and climbs trees and usually is located in the roof or upper stories of buildings if Norway rats are present.

Black rats are primarily active at night. They are good climbers and rarely form burrows. They are smaller and less aggressive than Norway rats and are usually forced to higher parts of buildings or are completely eliminated from areas by the Norway rat.

Norway Rat

Deborah Allen

Rattus norvegicus

Non-native

12 3/5" - 18 9/10" length
(32 - 48 cm)

8 9/10 - 19 oz
(280 - 540 g)

The back and the sides of the Norway rat are brown with scattered black hairs and the underside is pale gray or grayish brown. The fur is rather coarse looking. The tail is scaly and slightly shorter than the head and body length. The black rat has a longer tail and a darker body color. The ears are large, leaf-like, and naked. The Norway rat may be confused with the rice rat, which has softer looking fur, lighter undersides, and a slender tail. These Old World rats possess three rows of cusps on their upper molar teeth, which differs from the two rows observed in the native rats and mice.

◆ **STATUS & HABITAT**—The Norway or brown rat is one of the most common rodents associated with human habitation in the South. This species is absent from most of the park, with the possible exception of park buildings. It had been more common in some localities in the park because of past human habitation and agricultural activities. This rat is not native to the Americas and was introduced in the 1700s. It is considered a native of Japan and Asia. In the Americas the Norway rat occurs in every state in the United States and throughout most of the continent.

The Norway rat primarily inhabits buildings, grain fields, and garbage dumps. However, feral populations of these rats will occupy salt marshes. It is not a very agile climber and is usually located on the lower floors of buildings.

Two to 16 young are born per litter and these young can in turn breed when they are three months old. Up to eight litters are produced per year. Generally these rodents live one to three years in the wild. They are prey for snakes, foxes, weasels, and birds of prey.

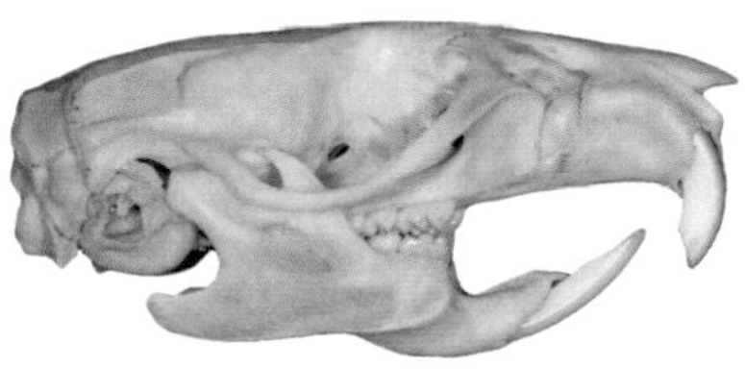

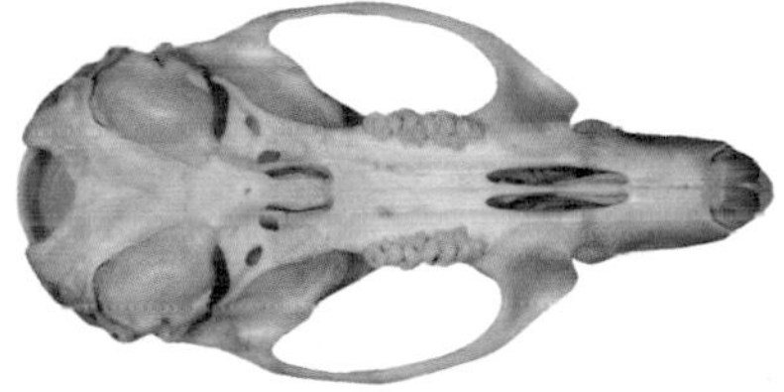

This species is one of the rats associated with the black plague in Europe. In the Americas, typhus fever, tularemia, rat-bite fever, leptosporosis, and Haverhill fever can be carried by this rodent.

Norway rats eat almost anything edible, with a preference for grain, seeds, and garbage. However, they will kill and eat insects, birds, and mammals.

These rodents are primarily active at night. They form extensive burrow systems and colonies consisting of up to 20 or more. They are larger and more aggressive than black rats and usually force the black rat to higher parts of buildings or completely eliminate them from an area.

House Mouse

Josef Hlasek

Mus musculus

Non-native

5 1/2" - 8" length
(14 - 20.5 cm)

1/2 - 1 oz
(14 - 28 g)

The back and the sides of the house mouse's body and head are grayish brown to brown and the underside is pale gray to buff white. The tail is scaly and slightly longer than the head and body length. The ears are large, leaf-like, and naked. The smell of the urine is very distinctive and very strong because of secretions from musk glands located near the anus.

◆ **STATUS & HABITAT**—The house mouse is one of the most common rodents associated with human habitation in the South and the world. This species is absent from most of the park with the possible exception of park buildings and fields. It once was more common in some localities in the park because of past human habitation and agricultural activities. This mouse is not native to the Americas and was introduced in the 1700s. It is considered a native of Eurasia. In the Americas the house mouse occurs in every state in the United States and throughout most of the continent.

Since the park is primarily forested and no longer farmed, suitable habitat and avenues for dispersal are limited. In buildings they can destroy woodwork, papers, and other important objects. Up to 13 young are born per litter and these young can in turn breed when they are one to two months old. Up to 13 litters are produced per year. Generally these rodents live one to two years in the wild. They are prey for snakes, foxes, weasels, and birds of prey.

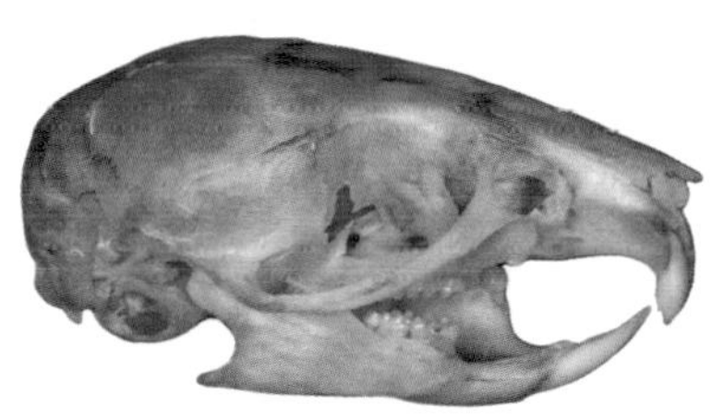

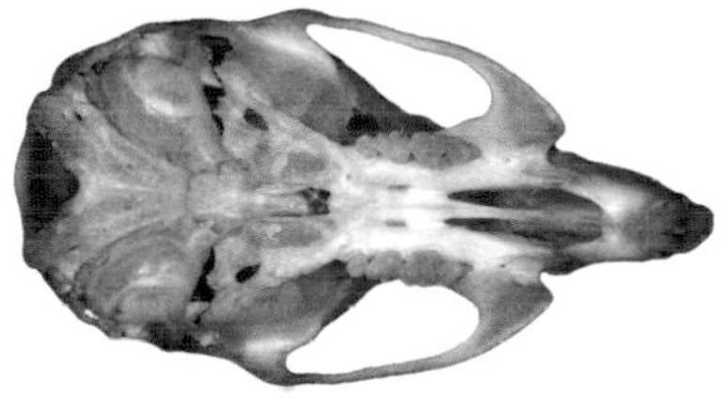

The house mouse primarily inhabits buildings, grain fields, and garbage dumps. However, feral populations of these mice will occupy fields and fencerows.

Virtually anything edible is eaten with preference given to grain, seeds, and garbage. However, they will eat roots, fungi and insects.

House mice are primarily active at night. They are agile climbers, swim well, and can form burrow systems. Studies have shown that the house mouse and the white-footed mouse are mutually antagonistic. This mouse constructs nests of shredded paper, fabric, and other soft materials within buildings, and nests of grass in burrow systems.

MEADOW JUMPING MOUSE

Phil Myers/Museum of Zoology, University of Michigan

Zapus hudsonius

7 1/10″ - 9 1/5″ length
(18 - 23.4 cm)

2/5 - 1 oz
(12 - 30 g)

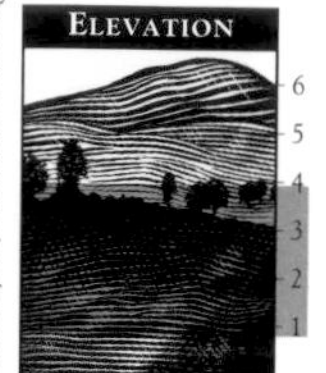

The sides of the head and body of this mouse are brownish yellow in color. A broad dorsal stripe runs down the head and back and is brownish yellow in coloration with blackish brown hairs intermixed. The feet and underparts are white to yellow and white on the sides. The sparsely haired tail is much longer than the body and is bi-colored, brown above and whitish below. The tail has a dark tuft of longer hairs at the tip and the fur is relatively coarse looking, diagnostic features that help distinguish this species from the woodland jumping mouse. Meadow jumping mice have enlarged hind legs that they use for jumping and relatively short, weak front feet.

◆ **STATUS & HABITAT**—The meadow jumping mouse is one of the more attractive small mammals in the park. It is rarely seen except when startled and bounding through the fields with leaps of up to 1 - 3 feet. This mouse is one of the smallest true hibernating rodents. It's primarily found in grassy fields, in brushy areas bordering fields, in thick vegetation near water, and in early successional-stage brushy areas. In the Americas the meadow jumping mouse occurs from southern Alaska across southern Canada to the Atlantic coast. This species' range extends from New England south to northern South Carolina and Georgia and west to Montana and Oklahoma.

The jumping activity of this species helps it elude predators. In addition, this species hibernates and thereby removes itself as a food resource for up to six months. Very little data exists on the predators of this species; however, weasels, skunks, mink, bobcat, snakes, and birds of prey are likely candidates. Population densities average 2 - 12 mice per acre. Usually two to eight young are born per litter. This mouse generally does not breed until 12 months of age. Up to two litters are produced per year. Generally these mice live one to two years in the wild.

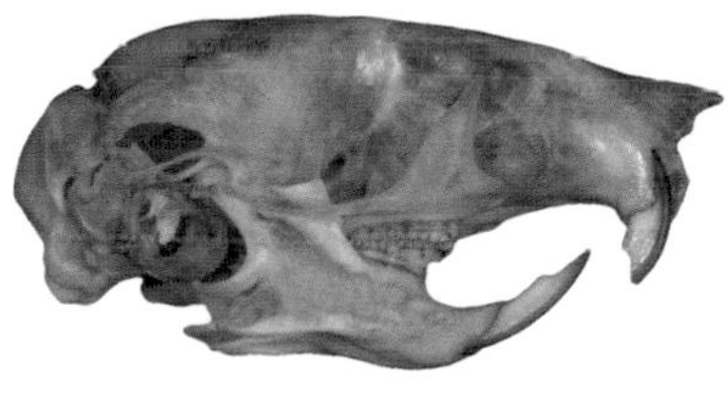

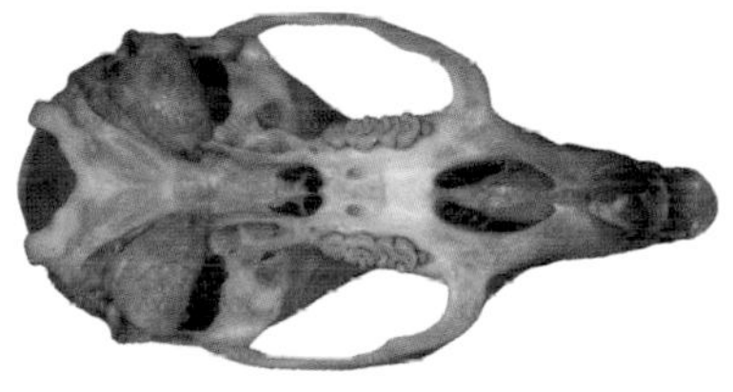

Favorite foods include fruits, nuts, insects, and other invertebrates. The subterranean fungus, genus *Endogone*, is a major food item.

Meadow jumping mice are nocturnal, but active during cloudy and rainy days. In the fall this species accumulates fat reserves that amount to about one-fourth of its body weight. Their hibernation extends from late October to April. This is one of the smallest true hibernators and body temperatures can fall to 5° C (40° F). These mice have nests that are located in brush piles, under fallen logs, or below ground. Some nests in winter may be 18 - 36 inches below ground. They are good climbers and use jumping activity primarily when startled.

Woodland Jumping Mouse

Phil Myers/Museum of Zoology, University of Michigan

Napaeozapus insignis

7 3/10" - 9 9/10" length
(18.5 - 25cm)

1/2 - 1 oz
(15 - 31 g)

The woodland jumping mouse is one of the most attractive small mammals in the park. The sides of the head and body are burnt-orange in color. A broad dorsal stripe runs down the back and is darker brown in coloration with dark tipped hairs. The feet and underparts are white. The tail is much longer than the body and bi-colored, brown above and whitish below. The tail usually has a white tuft of longer hairs at the tip, a diagnostic feature that helps distinguish this species from the meadow jumping mouse. It has enlarged hind legs that it uses for jumping and relatively short, weak front feet.

◆ **STATUS & HABITAT**—This species is primarily found at higher elevations. Forests with a heavy herbaceous layer and rhododendron thickets near water are excellent habitats.

In the Americas the woodland jumping mouse occurs throughout the southern sections of eastern Canada to the upper Midwest. This species' range extends from New England down the Appalachian Mountains to north Georgia.

This mouse is rarely seen and when startled is bounding through the woods with leaps of up to 12 feet. This mouse is one of the smallest true hibernating rodents.

The jumping activity of this species makes it more difficult for predators to capture. In addition, it hibernates and removes itself as a food resource for up to six months. Very little data exists on the predators of this species; however, weasels, skunks, mink, bobcat, snakes, and birds of prey probably eat it. Woodland jumping mice eat seeds, roots, fruits, insects and other invertebrates. The subterranean fungus, genus *Endogone*, is a major food item.

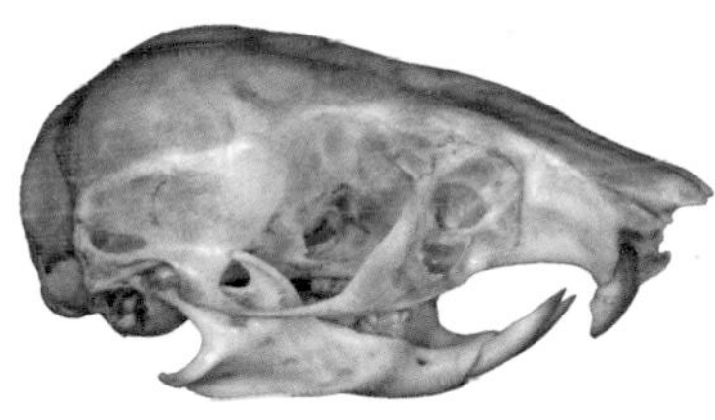

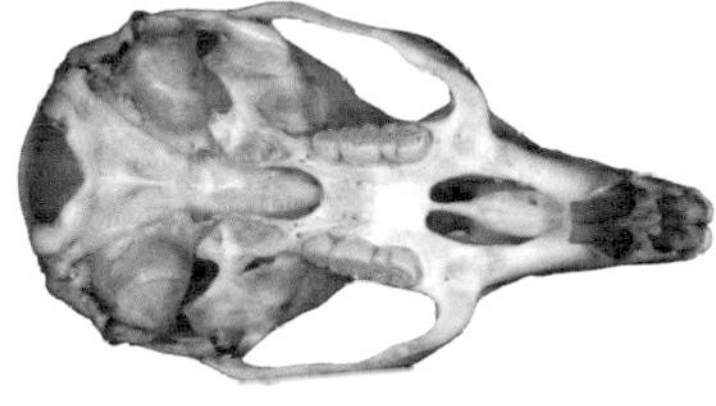

Population densities average five mice per acre, but little research has been done on this species and one study found 24 per acre. Usually two to seven young are born per litter. This species generally does not breed until 12 months of age. Up to two litters are produced per year. Generally these mice live two to six years in the wild.

This mouse is nocturnal. In the fall it accumulates fat reserves that amount to about one-third of its body weight. This fat serves as the main energy source for these mice during their deep hibernation period that extends from late October to April. During hibernation their body temperature can fall to 5° C (40° F). These mice have nests that are located in brush piles, under fallen logs, or below ground. They utilize other small mammal burrows and surface runways.

CARNIVORES

ORDER CARNIVORA

Canidae

Coyote
Red Wolf
Gray Wolf
Red Fox
Gray Fox

Ursidae

Black Bear

Procyonidae

Raccoon

Mustelidae

Long-tailed Weasel
Mink
Northern River Otter

Mephitidae

Eastern Spotted Skunk
Striped Skunk

Felidae

Mountain Lion
Bobcat

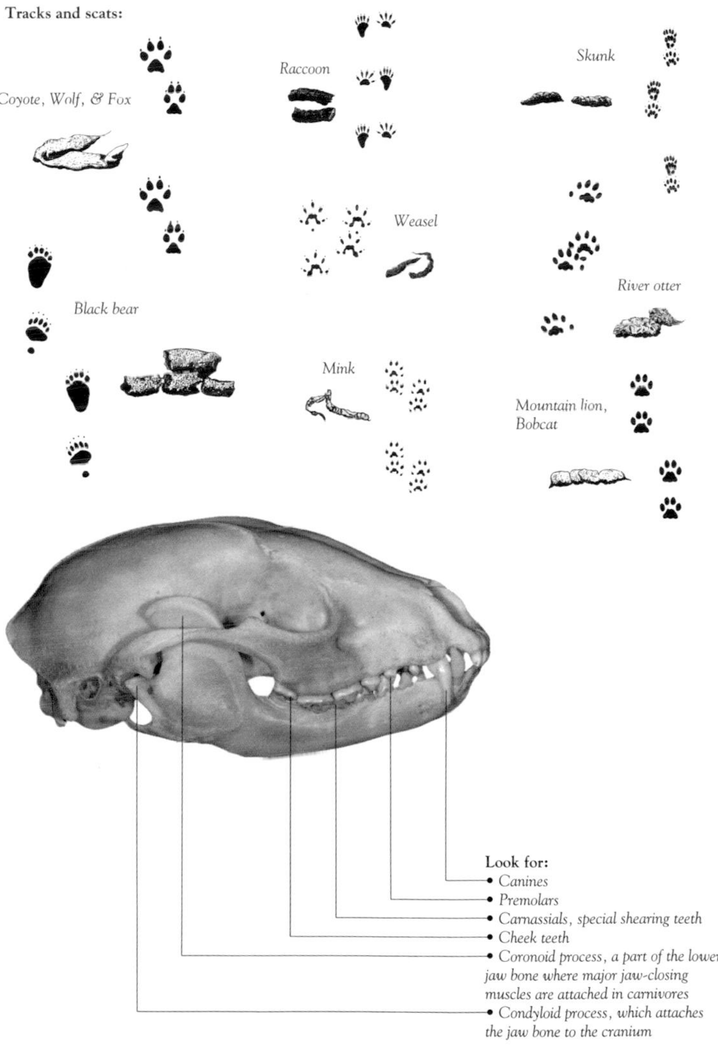
Tracks and scats:
Coyote, Wolf, & Fox
Raccoon
Skunk
Weasel
Black bear
River otter
Mink
Mountain lion, Bobcat
Look for:
• Canines
• Premolars
• Carnassials, special shearing teeth
• Cheek teeth
• Coronoid process, a part of the lower jaw bone where major jaw-closing muscles are attached in carnivores
• Condyloid process, which attaches the jaw bone to the cranium

Coyote

Bill Lea

Canis latrans

42″ - 47″ length
(108 - 120 cm)

Females: 22 - 29 lbs
(10 - 13 kg)
Males: 24 - 35 lbs
(11 - 16 kg)

Coyotes are variable in color, ranging from reddish to brown to yellowish to gray. The dorsal hairs are tipped in black and the abdomen and throat are light colored. Coyotes often are very difficult to distinguish from red wolves and gray wolves because all three species have variable color patterns. However, gray wolves and red wolves are considerably larger than coyotes and have a more massive body structure, particularly through the head, chest, legs, and feet.

◆ **STATUS & HABITAT**—The coyote is usually thought of as a Western species, but these animals began an eastward range expansion beginning in the 1940s. It has been hypothesized that red and gray wolves out-competed coyotes where their ranges met and, after wolves were extirpated, coyotes began their eastward trend. That range expansion was undoubtedly aided by forest clearing by humans, which created habitats more akin to those found in the West. Also, some coyotes were illegally transplanted by humans to Georgia, Florida, and perhaps other states. Coyotes were not known to exist in the Great Smoky Mountains until 1982, but anecdotal observations suggest their densities have gradually increased since they arrived.

Coyotes can now be found throughout most of North America, including all the eastern states. Although they may be found anywhere in the national park, coyotes prefer pastures, thickets, scrublands, and small woodlots. They usually hunt singly or sometimes in pairs and stalk their prey, relying on their vision, hearing, and sense of smell. They prey on a wide array of small to medium-sized mammals (rabbits, rats, and mice), and birds. Larger prey such as white-tailed deer fawns, wild hog piglets, and elk calves are also taken. Coyotes eat fruits and nuts as well, especially persimmons, grapes, and acorns.

Typically, five to 10 coyote pups are born in the spring following a 58- to 63-day gestation period. The young are weaned at about six weeks of age and the family group breaks up in the fall. Coyotes are more apt to travel alone or in pairs but can travel in small groups, although they are not highly structured packs as with gray wolves. Based on a study conducted in the early 1990s, home ranges of coyotes in the national park were large, ranging from 10 to 89 square miles (25 - 230 km^2). The smallest home range was for a coyote that centered its activity in Cades Cove, where prey densities are high.

Coyotes are often despised by farmers and ranchers, especially poultry and sheep growers. Coyotes are intelligent and adaptable, which often makes population control difficult. However, coyotes generally do not wreak the havoc often attributed to them. Their predation of farm animals is usually sporadic and minimal compared with other sources of livestock mortality.

© Dwight Kuhn

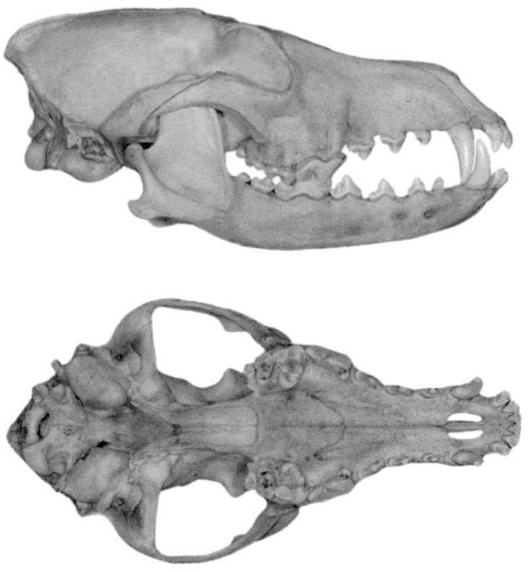

Red Wolf

Canis rufus

Extirpated

54" - 66"
(135 - 165 cm)

Females: 40 - 75 lbs
(18 - 34 kg)
Males: 50 - 85 lbs
(23 - 39 kg)

Bill Lea

The red wolf is an endangered species endemic to the southeastern U.S. It is intermediate in size compared with the larger gray wolf and the smaller coyote. It is very similar in appearance to the coyote, but its fur is more tawny-cinnamon colored, mixed with gray and black, and is darkest on the back. The tail has a black tip. A black color phase has been observed in the past. Like other members of the *Canidae* (dog family), red wolves walk on their toes (digitigrade).

◆ **STATUS & HABITAT**—Red wolves prefer forest margins, which provide access to vegetative cover and open fields where they hunt

Tom & Pat Leeson

for prey. Red wolves once occurred throughout the southeastern U.S., but are now relegated to one population in eastern North Carolina.

Red wolves do not form large packs like gray wolves, but typically form extended family groups of five to eight animals consisting of a breeding pair, pups, and juvenile animals. The mating season occurs in February and March and four to five pups are born about 63 days later in April or May. Pups usually are born in excavated earthen dens, hollow tree trunks, or under rock outcrops. Both the mother and father care for the pups, which become independent at six months. Red wolves can range widely, with home ranges varying from 20 to 40 square miles (50 - 100 km^2).

The red wolf was once on the brink of extinction. When only a handful of red wolves remained in the swamps of Louisiana and Texas during the 1960s, wildlife officials decided to capture all remaining animals before the population would become extinct. With only 14 pure red wolves left, a successful captive breeding program was initiated. Captive-bred animals were first released back into the wild in 1987 in Alligator River National Wildlife Refuge in eastern North Carolina. The first experimental release on an inland site was in the Cades Cove and Tremont areas of Great Smoky Mountains National Park in 1991 - 1996. Initial releases were encouraging and for a few years, visitors were able to hear the distinctive howl of the red wolf resonate through the night. However, the program was stopped in 1998 because survival of wild-born pups was low, wolves established home ranges outside the national park, and hybridization occurred with coyotes, which by then had become solidly established in the national park.

Red wolves hunt for white-tailed deer and medium-sized prey such as raccoons, rabbits, and woodchucks. During the experimental release in the Smokies, red wolves occasionally killed the non-native wild hog.

Gray Wolf

Dave Welling

Canis lupus

Extirpated

52" - 70" length
(130 - 180 cm)

Females: 40 - 120 lbs
(18 - 55 kg)
Males: 45 - 175 lbs
(20 - 80 kg)

Physically, gray wolves resemble a large domestic dog, except that wolves have longer legs, larger feet, and a narrower chest. Unlike many domestic dogs, the wolf's tail is straight. Color can range from pure white to gray to totally black. Gray wolves are considerably larger than coyotes and have a more massive body structure, particularly through the head, chest, legs, and feet.

◆ **STATUS & HABITAT**—The gray wolf is one of several large carnivores for which the Great Smoky Mountains were one of the last strongholds before they became extinct in the region. Although most authorities consider the gray wolf and the red wolf (*Canis rufus*) to be different species, there is some disagreement over which, or if both, occurred in the Great Smoky Mountains at the time of Euro-American settlement. The two species can interbreed and the southern Appalachians represent an area of historical overlap, with gray wolves generally distributed north of the Great Smoky Mountains and red wolves generally to the south (although red wolf remains have been recovered from archaeological sites in West Virginia and Virginia). Most early naturalists to the region refer to the wild canids they observed as gray wolves, but considerable confusion and disagreement remains about which species was present first, whether both occurred at the same time, and the amount of hybridization. Irrespective of the species, "wolves" were reported to be in the Great Smoky Mountains until about 1890; they were probably eradicated by humans soon after that.

The gray wolf remains primarily in northern areas of North America, including Canada, Alaska, and several northern states that border Canada. Recent reintroductions in Yellowstone National Park have been successful.

Wolves are highly social and normally live in packs, which have a strict social structure. Howling is used to assemble the pack and to

Richard Day/Daybreak Imagery

David Barron/Oxygen Group

maintain and defend the pack territory. A primary function of the wolf pack is to enable these animals to capture and kill large prey. In portions of its range where prey species are few, wolves can have a marked effect on prey populations and vice versa. In the Great Smoky Mountains, however, prey diversity was probably high enough that the effect of wolves on any one prey species was somewhat mediated. Home ranges of wolves in northern boreal forest can be as large as 1,200 square miles (3,100 km^2). Prey densities were likely higher in the southern Appalachians, so home ranges probably were smaller than in more northern regions.

Like domestic dogs, the gestation period of the gray wolf is 63 days. Average litter size is six.

Wolves are true carnivores and in the southern Appalachians they probably consumed large prey such as white-tailed deer and elk. Smaller prey, including rabbits and mice, were probably also eaten.

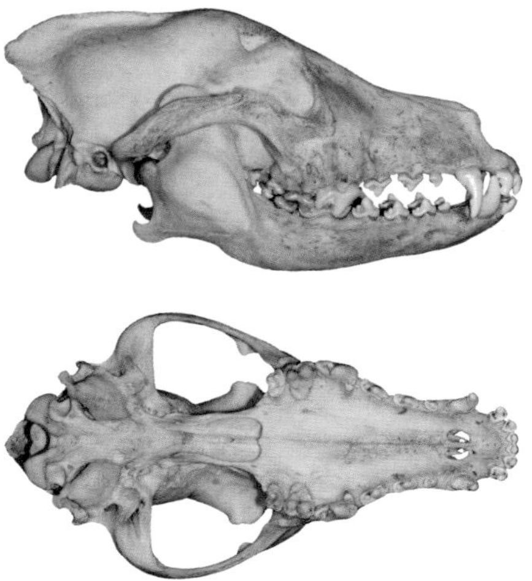

RED FOX

Vulpes vulpes

33″ - 44″ length
(82 - 110 cm)

8 - 12 lbs
(3.6 - 5.5 kg)

Tom & Pat Leeson

The red fox has relatively long legs and a slender appearance in contrast to all other fox species. Its upper body is reddish, its belly is white, and it has a large bushy tail. The tail has a white tip, which distinguishes it from all other North American canids. The lower legs and feet are black.

◆ **STATUS & HABITAT**—Except for humans, this canid has the distinction of being one of the most widely distributed terrestrial mammals in the world. Red foxes have adapted to such diverse habitats as arctic tundra, deciduous forests, semiarid deserts, as well as agricultural and urban landscapes.

There is a long-standing controversy among scientists as to whether this canid is truly native to North America or whether it was introduced by European-American settlers during the 1700s. As gray and red wolves disappeared from large portions of their former range, red foxes colonized these areas. Red foxes now occupy all but the most arid parts of North America.

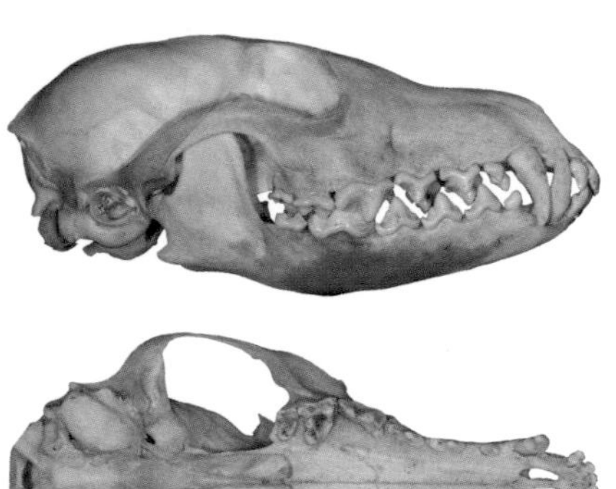

Breeding takes place in late winter with a gestation period of 50 to 55 days. Young pups are born in an earthen den and litter sizes average four to six young. Home ranges of red foxes vary with habitat quality and season and range from a few hundred acres to several square miles. Red foxes appear to be more territorial than gray foxes. Both species mark with urine and feces along travel routes and home range boundaries. During field research studies in the national park, hundreds of fox scats (gray and red) were collected along hiking trails. These scats were found at all elevations and habitat types.

The diet of red foxes varies with seasonal food availability. The relatively long legs and slender body enhances their mobility and allows the species to exploit more open habitats and larger prey than gray foxes. This partially compensates for the less omnivorous diet of

Dave Welling

the red fox compared with the gray fox. Prey of red foxes includes rabbits, rodents, fruits, eggs, carrion, and domesticated animals such as chickens, piglets, and lambs. Red foxes are known to cache surplus food, returning periodically to feed.

Mortality of red foxes is similar to that of gray foxes (distemper, rabies, road kills, coyotes, bobcats, and dogs). Sarcoptic mange is also a noteworthy cause of mortality in red foxes. Life span averages four to six years with few red foxes living more than eight years. Young red foxes are occasionally observed "panhandling" along roadsides in Great Smoky Mountains National Park. Do not feed them!

GRAY FOX

Bill Lea

Urocyon cinereoargenteus

32″ - 40″ length
(80 - 100 cm)

6 - 9 lbs
(2.7 - 3.6 kg)

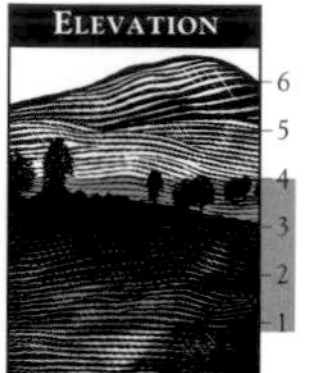

The gray fox has a black-tipped tail, gray back, rusty-cinnamon sides and legs, and a dark stripe down the center of the back. The stocky appearance and relatively short legs distinguish this fox from the red fox. These characteristics, accompanied by long, sharp, semi-retractable, recurved claws and the ability to rotate forelimbs more than any other canid, enable gray foxes to climb trees. Consequently, the species' other common name is the tree fox. Grasping a tree trunk with forelegs and pushing with hind feet enables the gray fox to climb and escape predators and gain access to tree fruits, such as persimmons. This latter event was recorded during field studies in the Cades Cove area of the park in the 1970s.

◆ **STATUS & HABITAT**—The gray fox occurs throughout the U.S., except in the northern Rocky Mountains, and ranges south through Mexico and Central America. Gray foxes feed on a variety of prey, including cottontail rabbits and small rodents as well as fruit, nuts, insects, and carrion. Although gray foxes are regarded as the most woodland dependent of all the fox species, they do well where forest and agricultural areas are mixed. For example, night-light surveys of fields in Cades Cove revealed just as many gray foxes using the fields as red foxes. Home ranges of both species overlap, but they appear to avoid confrontations.

Gray and red foxes have been affected by the appearance of coyotes in Great Smoky Mountains National Park. Coyotes are known to kill foxes, displace them from favored habitats, and compete for prey. The tree climbing ability of gray foxes and their more omnivorous food habits may have given them an advantage over red foxes in the presence of coyotes. Scats of gray and red foxes are usually indistinguishable, but smaller than coyote scats, ½ inch versus greater than ¾ inch diameter, respectively. Other mortality factors on gray foxes include predation by bobcats, distemper, rabies, and human causes (vehicle collisions, trapping, and shooting). Most gray foxes die before four years of age, with an occasional individual surviving to 10.

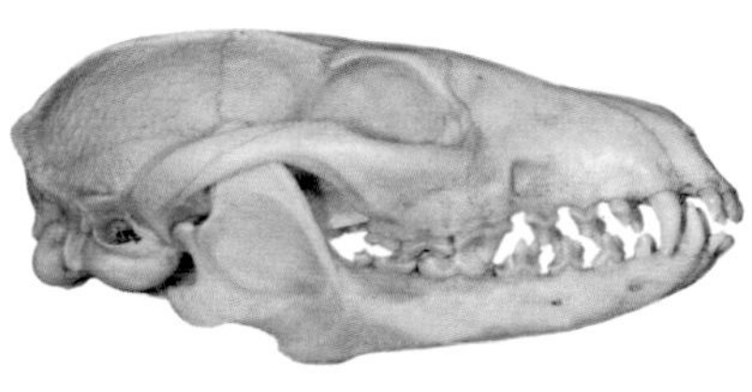

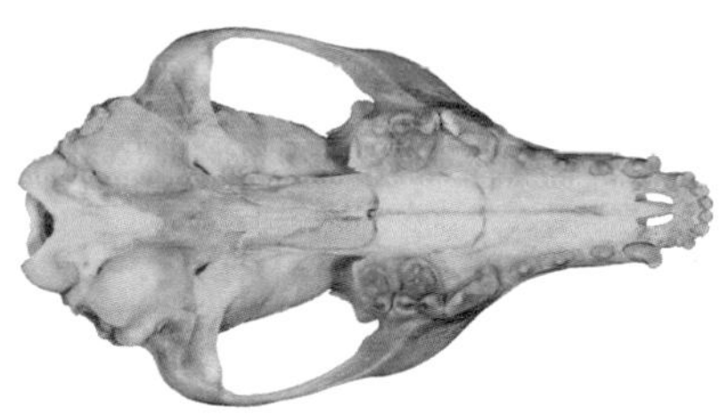

Female gray foxes typically use earthen dens as a birthing site. Dens are excavated or modified from burrows of other species, such as woodchucks. The normal litter size is three to four pups, which are born in March-April. As with most canids, gray foxes are crepuscular—nocturnal in their activity. Annual home ranges cover 200 - 2,000 acres, varying with season and habitat quality.

American Black Bear

Bill Lea

Ursus americanus

Adult females: 56″ length (140 cm)
Adult males: 64″ length (160 cm)

Adult females: 90 - 130 lbs (61 - 59 kg)
Adult males: 200 - 300 lbs (91 - 136 kg)

The black bear is always black in the Great Smokies, with a brown muzzle and occasionally a small, white chest blaze.

◆ **STATUS & HABITAT**—This remarkable large mammal is embedded in the lore, legends, and legacy of Great Smoky Mountains National Park. No other animal enjoys the status of this charismatic species. It has been the symbol of the national park since its establishment in 1934. Few animals captivate the interest of visitors like black bears. Due to logging, human settlement, and the loss of the American chestnut to a blight, black bears were almost extirpated

Bill Lea

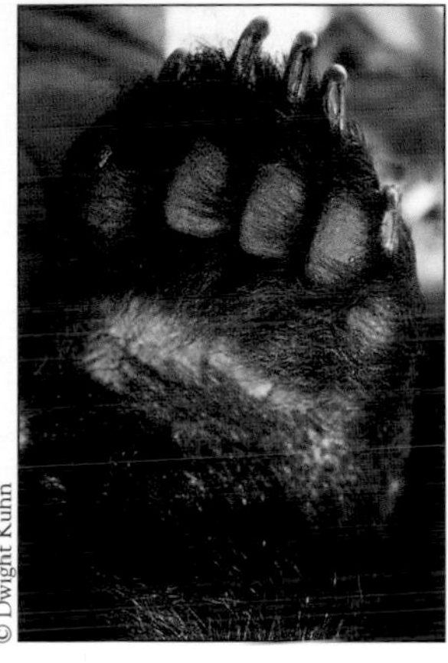
© Dwight Kuhn

prior to establishment of the national park. The population has since recovered and presently there are over two bears per square mile, or 1,400 - 1,800, in the national park, one of the highest densities throughout its range.

Black bears are omnivores and feed on seasonally available foods. They consume squawroot, a parasitic plant that grows from the roots of oak trees, and herbaceous plant materials in the spring. In summer, they feed on blueberries, huckleberries, and blackberries, which are referred to as soft mast. During fall, bears forage extensively in preparation for winter denning, and weights may increase by as much as 25 - 50% due to consumption of large amounts of hard mast such as acorns, hickory nuts, and beechnuts. In years of low acorn yield in the Great Smoky Mountains, bears will focus on alternative foods such as grapes.

Black bears are very intelligent mammals, probably second only to primates. This noteworthy attribute, along with their keen sense of smell, agility, strength, speed, and climbing ability, results in a formidable animal. Dealing with human-bear interactions is a continuous challenge for park managers. However, in recent years, much has been done to prevent human-bear interactions. Park managers have incorporated larger bear-proof dumpsters, boosted public education materials, closed picnic areas earlier, changed work schedules of employees, and installed food storage cable systems for backcountry campers. Managers have also been more proactive in dealing with nuisance bears and have employed innovative management techniques for potential problem bears.

Adult females are four years or older when they breed for the first time. They typically breed every other year in mid summer. Implantation of the fertilized egg, however, is delayed until late November. Female bears go into winter dens in early to late December and emerge in April or early May. Typically, two cubs are born in late January or early February. Young stay with the mother for 18 months before they disperse. Males have a much shorter denning period.

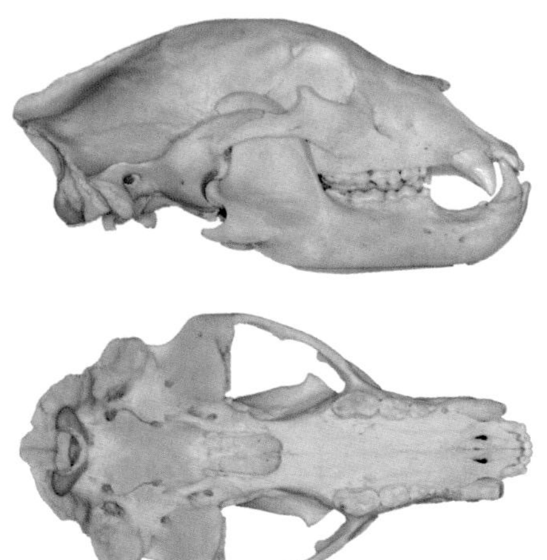

The oldest documented black bear ages in the national park were 26 years for a female and 20 years for a male. Mortality is typically human-related, as black bears have no natural predators in the Smokies.

Procyon lotor

24″ - 38″ length
(60 - 95 cm)

8 - 14 lbs
(3.6 - 6.4 kg)

Bill Lea

The raccoon is a medium-sized mammal with distinctly omnivore attributes such as wide, flat crushing molar teeth, while retaining the typical enlarged canines characteristic of all carnivores. The most striking identifying features are the black mask and ringed tail, hence its nickname "masked bandit." Dark guard hairs cover a lighter thick underfur. Raccoons walk on the flat of their feet (plantigrade). Their naked footpads and toes resemble a human print. Although raccoons have keen senses of smell, vision, and hearing, they also use their highly sensitized front feet to locate and capture food.

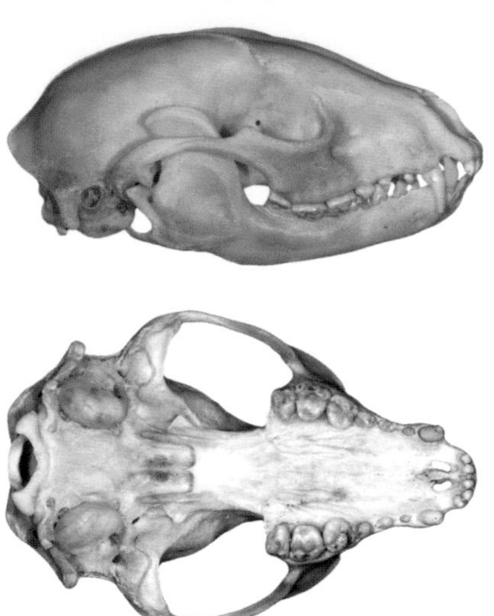

◆ **STATUS & HABITAT**—This intelligent carnivore is mostly nocturnal and usually makes its presence known wherever it resides. Raccoons are adaptable, persistent and curious mammals that thrive remarkably well in developed neighborhoods as well as natural areas. While entertaining to some, other people must deal with constant nuisance activity, usually associated with human food or garbage. This problem is particularly true where raccoon populations are protected, such as in the national park around picnic areas and campgrounds.

Field studies of raccoons in the national park revealed that large red oak trees were preferred refuge sites but rock crevices were also commonly used. Communal winter denning was frequently observed, providing a convenient strategy for heat conservation. Of 135 park raccoons that researchers aged, only 12 were older than four years; seven years was the oldest documented age. In unprotected populations, average ages are likely younger. Besides mortality caused by humans (hunting, dogs, and vehicle collisions), raccoons succumb to predation by coyotes and bobcats and diseases such as rabies and canine distemper. Distemper was documented in one section of the national park in the early 1980s, resulting in a population decline of over 75% in less than three months.

Raccoons occur throughout North America, except for northern Canada and Alaska, and range as far south as Central America. They are attracted to the edges of streams, ponds, lakes, or marshes in both remote and urban landscapes. They prey on many aquatic species, such as frogs and crayfish. Also, nests of birds and turtles are vulnerable to raccoons. Acorns are preferred in fall and facilitate buildup of fat reserves before winter.

Breeding usually occurs in March or April with a 63-day gestation period. An average of three to four young are born in secure tree cavities. Home ranges average 200 - 500 acres. Often, home ranges are linear in shape because they are associated with stream courses. Raccoons are excellent climbers and are particularly attracted to large trees for escape, resting places, and winter and natal den sites.

© Dwight Kuhn

Raccoons have characteristically striped tails.

LONG-TAILED WEASEL

© Dwight Kuhn

Mustela frenata

12″ - 16″ length; tail is 70% of total length (30 - 40 cm)

Females: 2.8 - 8.8 oz (80 - 250 g)
Males: 5.6 - 15.8 oz (160 - 450 g)

The long-tailed weasel is the smallest carnivore in Great Smoky Mountains National Park. Like other weasels, it has a long, slender body and a small head with small rounded ears, all adaptations that allow them to enter the small hiding places of their prey. In summer, the upper body is dark brown and the lower body is a yellowish white. The tail is entirely brown, except for a black tip. In northern latitudes, the color changes in winter to white, but in the Great Smoky Mountains that change is more subtle to a buff brown color. The tip of the tail remains black.

◆ **STATUS & HABITAT**—Suitable habitats for the long-tailed weasel include areas close to cover with large and diverse populations of small mammals and birds. They seem to prefer habitats in close proximity to waterways and standing water. Foraging occurs along borders of pastures, old fields, or natural edge habitats. Dens are usually located in dense, brushy vegetation.

Long-tailed weasel home ranges are 25 - 60 acres (10 - 24 ha), depending on season and availability of prey. Home ranges tend to be smaller in winter, when weasels need to conserve energy. Males and females are mostly solitary but portions of their home ranges overlap. Because of the small size and elongated body, long-tailed weasels have a high metabolism and are highly active day and night searching for prey. Like other mustelids, long-tailed weasels move in a series of gallops, arching their back with each bound. They use their keen sense of smell and hearing to locate prey. In pursuit of prey, they have been

© Dwight Kuhn

observed swimming, climbing trees, and tunneling through snow. Although rarely seen, their scat is very characteristic (1" - 2" long, thin, and very twisted with tapered ends) and is occasionally seen along trails. Foxes and birds of prey, particularly owls, are the primary predators of long-tailed weasels.

The breeding season is from July through August. The implantation of the fertilized eggs in the uterine wall is delayed by about eight months. The gestation period is 27 days, so the 4 - 5 pups are usually born in April or May of the next year.

Small to medium-sized rodents and rabbits are their primary prey, but long-tailed weasels also pursue small birds, bird eggs, and even small reptiles.

The long-tailed weasel has the largest range of any mustelid in the Western Hemisphere and occurs from southern Canada to northern Bolivia in South America. Within the U.S., distribution is throughout, with the exception of arid regions in the Southwest.

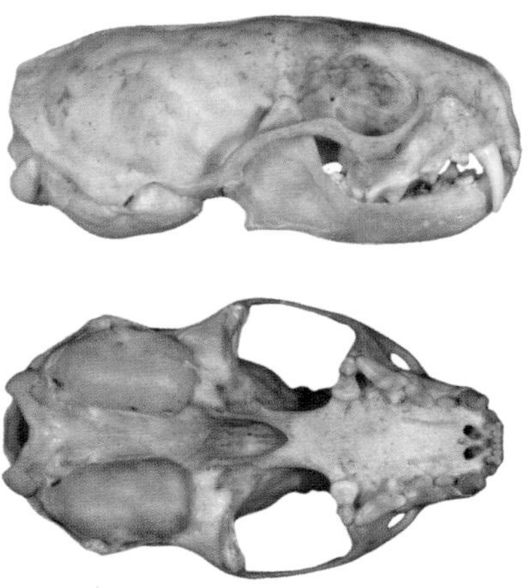

Linda Freshwaters Arndt

Mustela vison

Females: 18″ - 23″
(460 - 575 mm)
1.5 - 2.4 lbs
(0.7 - 1.1 kg)

Males: 23″ - 28″ length
(580 - 700 mm)
2.0 - 3.5 lbs
(0.9 - 1.6 kg)

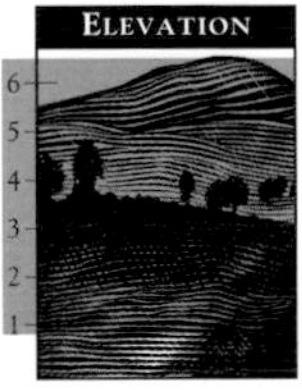

Mink are found in Great Smoky Mountains National Park, but their elusive behavior makes it difficult to know how common they are here. Mink have dark chocolate-colored guard hairs underlain by dense underfur that is slightly lighter in color. This fur keeps them warm while in the water, but will dry quickly once on land. This same characteristic also makes mink a highly desired furbearing animal. The head, feet, and tip of the tail of the mink can be almost black. Mink will commonly have a white mark on the chest or chin.

Mink are extremely inquisitive and intelligent. In 2006 a mink had to be killed at the

Ronald Phillips

Oconaluftee Mountain Farm Museum after it killed several chickens and charged a park ranger!

Although mink are not as aquatic as river otters, they can swim well. Mink have been known to dive to depths of over 15 feet (5 m) and can swim underwater for a distance of 100 feet (30 m). Their feet are semi-webbed and are completely furred except for the toe and sole pads.

◆ **STATUS & HABITAT**—Mink have a high metabolic rate and, consequently, must eat frequently. Mink will eat small mammals, fish, birds, amphibians, crustaceans, insects, and reptiles. All these food items are eaten with more or less equal frequency. Of mammals eaten, the most common species are mice, muskrats, and rabbits. Blackbirds, waterfowl, songbirds, and eggs are the most common bird species consumed. Frogs, crayfish, and a wide variety of fish are other important

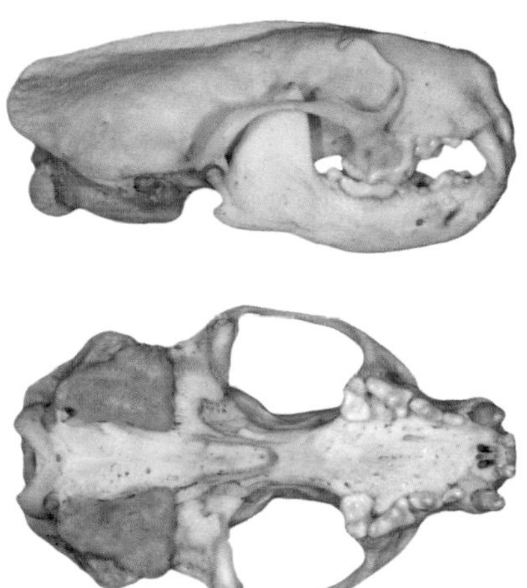

food items. There seems to be some segregation of food items taken by mink according to sex, with males consuming relatively larger prey than females. Mink habitat consists of virtually any watercourse in Great Smoky Mountains National Park where there is sufficient cover and seclusion. Males may require a stream stretch of about 1.6 miles (2.6 km) and females may occupy a 1.1 mile-stretch (1.8 km). Mink live throughout Canada, Alaska, the eastern U.S., and northern portions of the Midwest.

Mink mate from January through March with birth occurring 40-75 days after mating, depending on the length of the delayed implantation period. Litter sizes range from one to ten and average about four. Mink are susceptible to environmental contaminants and population reductions due to mercury, PCBs, and pesticides have been documented.

Northern River Otter

Michael Quinton

Lontra canadensis

Reintroduced

36″ - 50″
(91.5 - 127.0 cm)

11 - 30 lbs
(5 - 14 kg)

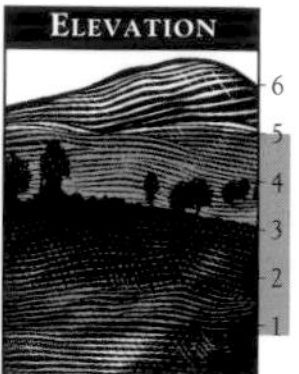

Northern river otters are seldom seen, but their tracks and scats can be easily found in Abrams Creek and in many other watersheds in the national park. Otter slides in fresh snow have been observed along the Middle Prong of the Little River. Otters have short, dense fur ranging in color from a rich chocolate brown to pale brown. They have a long tail, thick at the base, which facilitates swimming. Their toes are webbed and their body is torpedo-shaped, which also helps in swimming.

◆ **STATUS & HABITAT**—Northern river otters once were common in the lower elevation watersheds of the Great Smoky Mountains, but unregulated harvest and habitat deterioration led to their extirpation. The last historic river otter sighting in the Smokies was in 1936. In 1986, 11 river otters obtained in coastal North Carolina were released at Abrams Creek in Cades Cove to test whether reintroduction was feasible. Those releases were successful and 14 more river otters from South Carolina and Louisiana were released in the Little River in 1988, followed by the release of 100 Louisiana otters throughout the national park in 1994. Upon release, some otters moved remarkable distances (up to 118 miles; 190 km) over rough terrain; one otter was even observed by a ranger along the Appalachian Trail.

River otters prefer secluded, wooded streams with abundant bank debris such as rocks and logs. River otters occur throughout the U.S. and Canada, except in polar and desert regions.

Otters can dive to a depth of 60 feet (20 m) and swim for distances of up to 1/4 mile (400 m) without coming up for air. Like most members of the weasel family, river otters exhibit delayed implantation, with breeding and ovulation occurring in late winter. Average litter sizes are two to three. Otters are intelligent and their ability to make a game of almost any activity is well known. Otters have an acute sense of smell and highly developed tactile senses. Their hearing is good, but they are

Bill Lea

nearsighted, an adaptation for underwater vision.

Otters are sensitive to environmental pollutants because some contaminants remain in the aquatic food chain for many years. Accumulation of those pollutants probably contributed to their early extirpation. Otters have benefited from the resurgence of beavers in the Southeast because beaver ponds provide ideal otter habitat.

Food habits of otters are easy to study because they routinely deposit scats at specific locations, called latrines. Otters feed on a wide variety of fish and invertebrates. Examination of otter scat has revealed that crayfish represented the most important food for otters in Great Smoky Mountains National Park, followed by fish species such as white suckers, stonerollers, and northern hogsuckers. Fish eaten by river otters tend to be slow swimmers.

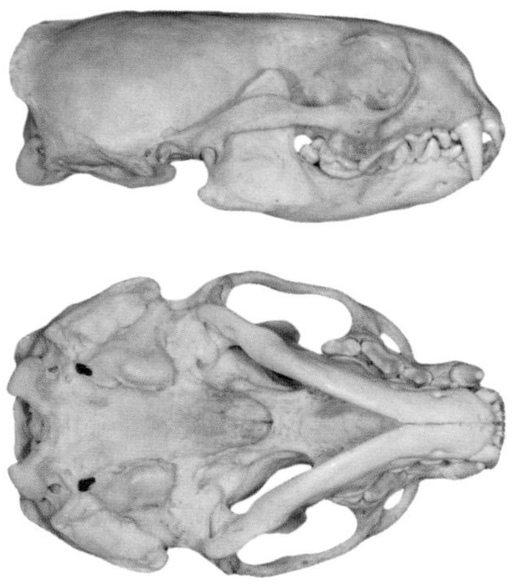

Bob Gress

Spilogale putorius

18″ - 22″ length
(45 - 55 cm)
Males are approximately 10% larger than females

Females: 16 oz
(450 g)
Males: 25 oz
(700 g)

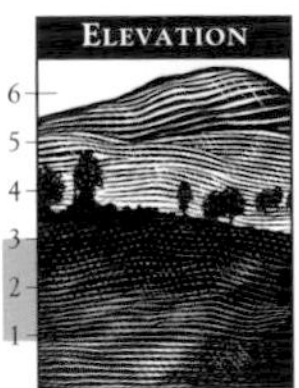

The eastern spotted skunk is a rare carnivore that is seldom seen in the national park. Locally known as "civet" or "civet cat," this species is much smaller than the striped skunk. It can also be distinguished from its larger cousin by the white spots that appear as six broken stripes on black, dense fur. Spotted skunks have a white nose patch in the shape of a triangle as well as small white spots in front of the ears and one on the forehead. They are agile tree climbers and are more nocturnal and alert than striped skunks.

◆ **STATUS & HABITAT**—Throughout their range, very few sightings of spotted skunks are reported. Besides being highly secretive, they occur in very low densities. Sightings in the national park have been primarily at low to middle elevations, including Cades Cove, park service headquarters area, Cataloochee Valley, Greenbrier Cove, and other locations that contain the edge habitats that spotted skunks prefer.

These skunks are found from the Midwest to the southeastern states and north into the central Appalachians. Their diet is very similar to that of striped skunks and consists mainly of beetles and other insects, rodents and rabbits, worms, bird eggs, and, on occasion, fruit. Spotted skunks prefer edge habitats, such as the fields of Cades Cove, where it uses fencerows, barn areas, tall grasslands, and wood edges.

Their breeding season is from late March through late April. Upon mating, the implantation of fertilized eggs in the uterine wall is delayed by 30 days. They produce a litter of two to six young after a gestation period of about 60 to 70 days. The young weigh less than a half ounce (10 grams) at birth and are hairless. Similar to the striped skunk, when threatened the spotted skunk may spray musk from their two anal glands. Rather than spraying, however, they will often attempt to intimidate opponents by charging and doing "handstands" on their front legs, which makes them appear larger. Like black bears, they will often stamp their feet repeatedly on the ground. As a last resort they will spray musk, which contains mercaptan, a chemical that produces the highly pungent odor. The odor of spotted skunks is stronger than that of striped skunks. Natural predators of spotted skunk include Great Horned Owls, bobcats, and domestic pets. Most mortality is human-caused and occurs in the form of automobile collisions and shooting.

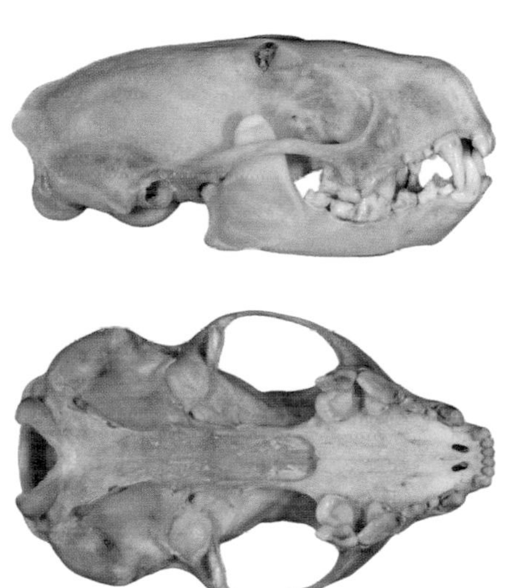

Striped Skunk

Bill Lea

This medium-sized carnivore is easily identified and well known, but not particularly well liked by humans. The distinctive black fur, dorsal white stripes, and bushy tail are sufficient warning to potential enemies that this relatively slow and gentle mammal is a noteworthy adversary. There are two well-developed scent glands on either side of the anus, each containing about ½ ounce of an oily, sulfur-alcohol compound called butylmercaptan. If sufficiently threatened, striped

Mephitis mephitis

21″ - 31″ length
(52 - 77 cm)

2 - 4 lbs
(0.9 - 1.8 kg)

Elevation

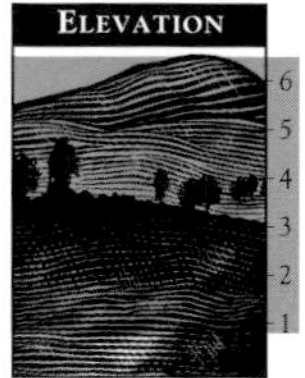

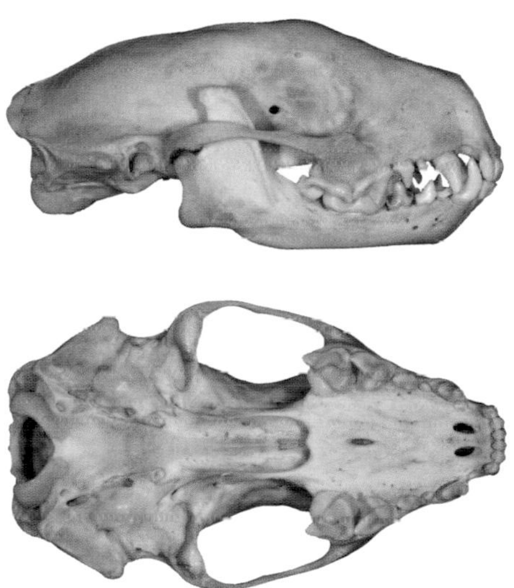

skunks are capable of spraying this powerful scent eight to ten feet.

◆ **STATUS & HABITAT**—Striped skunks adapt readily to humans. In the past, campgrounds and picnic areas in Great Smoky Mountains National Park were routinely patrolled by skunks foraging or panhandling for food and garbage. A two-year field study in the Cades Cove Picnic Area and Campground resulted in the capture of over 150 skunks. As long as they are not threatened, skunks maintain an air of "dignified indifference" toward national park visitors.

Breeding takes place in late winter. Litters of five to seven young are born in ground dens. Dens consist of stumps, fallen trees, or woodchuck cavities and are used as both summer and winter refuges.

Home ranges vary according to food availability and may be as small as 100 acres to over 700 acres. High mortality causes a rapid turnover in striped skunks, with most dying in less than a year; few reach four or five years of age. Besides human-caused mortality, Great Horned Owls are a significant predator as well as bobcat, coyote, and foxes. Skunks also are a major vector for rabies and succumb to distemper and a variety of other bacterial and viral diseases. Visitors to Great Smoky Mountains National Park should avoid confrontations with this mammal no matter how docile and friendly they seem. Never attempt to feed skunks or other park wildlife.

Striped skunks are normally nocturnal and use a wide variety of habitats. They spend their active hours foraging, primarily for insects, but also for a variety of small invertebrates (earthworms), vertebrates (rodents), and wild fruits (blackberries). The successful survival strategy of skunks and their broad omnivorous diet have allowed this species to occupy a variety of habitats throughout North America, including urban areas.

MOUNTAIN LION

Erwin & Peggy Bauer

Puma concolor
Extirpated
6.5′ - 7.5′ length
(2.0 - 2.3 m)

Females: 77 - 100 lbs
(35 - 45 kg)
Males: 120 - 146 lbs
(55 - 66 kg)

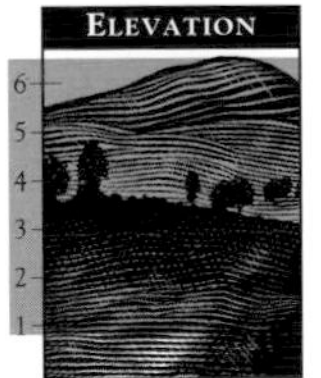

Mountain lions are the largest cat in North America and have short tawny-colored fur on the dorsal surface of the body, and lighter colored fur underneath. The subspecies of mountain lion that historically occurred in the southern Appalachians was the eastern cougar (*Puma concolor couguar*). The last verified record of a mountain lion in the Great Smoky Mountains was in 1920 of an animal that attacked a sheep herder on Spence Field. The mountain lion was subsequently killed near what is now Fontana Village.

◆ **STATUS & HABITAT**—The presence of mountain lions in Great Smoky Mountains

National Park and elsewhere in the Appalachian Mountains has been the subject of much debate. Sightings of large cats are routinely reported by the public but none have been verified. However, given the lack of any definitive evidence to the contrary, one must conclude that the eastern cougar is extinct. Occasional sightings could be the result of escaped or released captive animals. Mountain lions are solitary and nocturnal. Young are born in the spring and summer and usually consist of two to three kittens.

Although virtually any habitat that can support its prey is suitable mountain lion habitat, human intolerance generally prohibits the reestablishment of mountain lions. Illegal killing was a major impediment to mountain lion reestablishment in areas of northern Florida where they were reintroduced. Mountain lion habitat in Great Smoky Mountains National Park is probably suitable if humans would tolerate them. Changing long-held human beliefs about large predators would be an immense challenge.

Mountain lions prey mainly on white-tailed deer and elk. In the Smokies, deer densities are relatively low except in cleared areas like Cades Cove and Cataloochee Valley, so historic mountain lion densities probably were not high. Today, non-nativ European wild boars and feral hogs are common and could help sustain a mountain lion population.

Despite habitat fragmentation, the mountain lion still has a very extensive range, from southern Chile and Argentina to southeastern Alaska. Its current range in North America is primarily in unpopulated areas of the West, although populations have expanded east in recent years as far as Missouri. A relict population of probably less than 100 mountain lions still exists in south Florida, representing the only population of the subspecies *Puma concolor coryi*, the Florida panther.

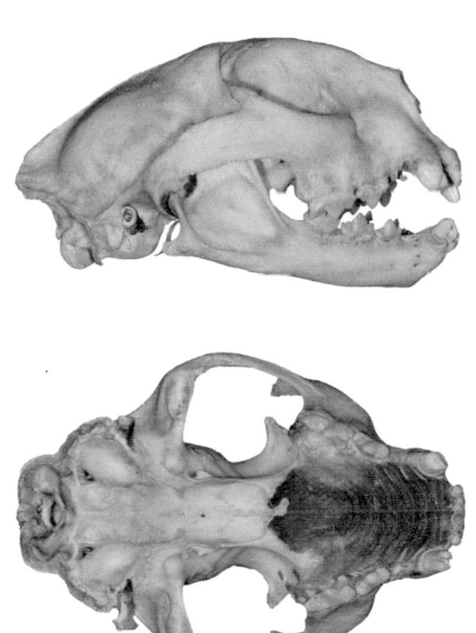

BOBCAT

Bill Lea

Lynx rufus

28″ - 40″ length
(70 - 100 cm)

Females: 20 lbs
(9 kg)
Males: 26.5 lbs
(12 kg)

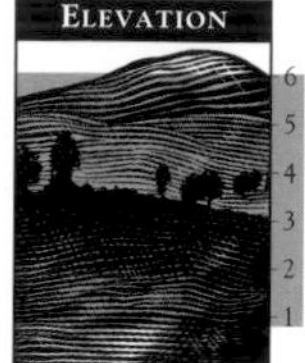

The bobcat is a medium-sized member of the cat family (*Felidae*) that occurs throughout the national park. It is rarely seen because of its highly secretive behavior and excellent camouflage. The fur on its back and side is light to dark brown with black streaks and spots. The short tail has distinct black bands on the upper side but is white below, a characteristic that distinguishes bobcats from lynx (*Lynx canadensis*). Besides the short tail, bobcats can be distinguished from domestic cats because they are larger, have long legs, and have prominent ears, which may have a distinct black tuft. Although they are generally quiet, loud yowls or meows may be heard, particularly during the breeding season.

◆ **STATUS & HABITAT**—Bobcats live in a wide variety of habitats in Great Smoky Mountains National Park, but prefer rocky or brushy areas where forests border open habitats. Those areas have high densities of their principal prey species—the cottontail rabbit—and provide den sites and cover. Bobcats are known to kill deer fawns on occasion. Prey are sometimes cached or covered.

Bobcats range from southern Canada throughout the entire United States, except for several mid-western states. The range overlaps only slightly with that of the lynx, whose larger paws provide them a competitive advantage when traveling and hunting in deep snow.

Bobcats typically occur at low densities but are widespread throughout the area, including areas near human developments. Adult bobcats typically maintain a distinct home range of 0.4 - 1.9 square miles (1 - 5 km^2), with males covering a larger area than females. Juvenile bobcats are transient and will set up a home range once a

Bill Lea

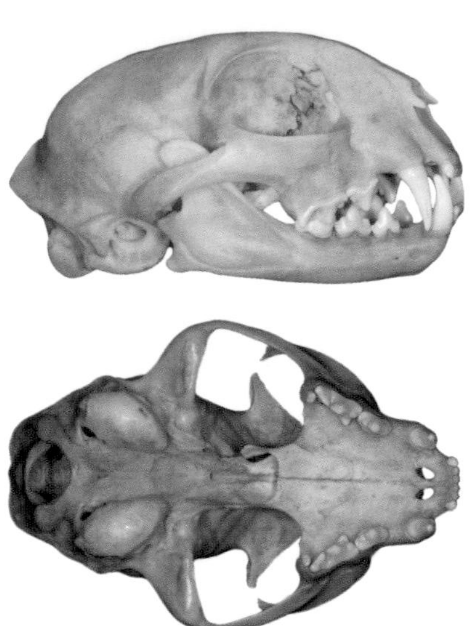

resident animal dies or leaves. Social organization among bobcats is likely maintained by scent marking using urine, feces, or secretions from anal glands. Those areas are usually at distinct locations, and are frequently found along the side of a trail at a switchback or on a rock or log. Bobcats are seen only rarely and are thought to have low densities. However, a research project on coyotes in the Cades Cove area in 1990–1991 unexpectedly resulted in 10 captures of bobcats, more than those of coyotes, an indication that we know very little about this elusive cat.

The bobcat breeding season peaks in March, followed by a gestation period of around 60 days. Two to three young are born in dens (rock crevices or ledges, brush piles, hollow trees), are weaned at two months, and become independent in fall or early winter.

Hoofed Mammals

ORDER ARTIODACTYLA

Family Suidae

European Wild Hog

Family Cervidae

Elk
White-tailed Deer

Family Bovidae

American Bison

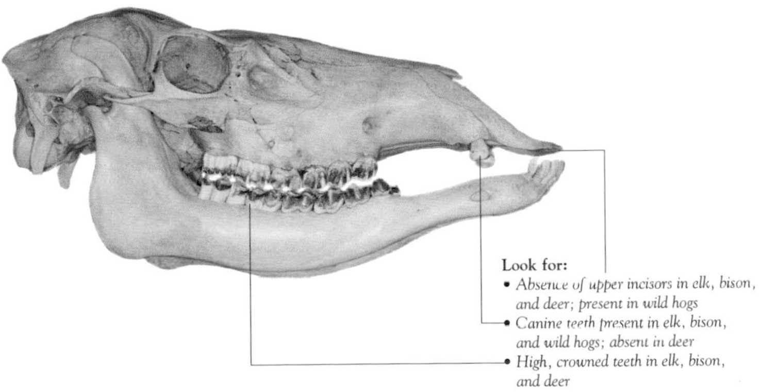

Tracks and scats:

European Wild Hog

Elk

White-tailed Deer

American Bison

European Wild Hog

Bil Lea

Sus scrofa

Non-native

39″ - 60″ length
(100 - 150 mm)
30″ - 36″ height
(76 - 92 mm)

70 - 350 lbs
(30 - 136 kg)

European wild boars, wild hogs, feral hogs, and domestic hogs are all the same species (*Sus scrofa*). Wild hogs in Great Smoky Mountains National Park are a hybrid of European wild boars and domestic hogs. They have most of the physical characteristics of wild boar, including thick bristly hair and mostly black coloration, but in more recent years an increasing number of animals are brown, spotted, or have white hair on their face and legs—characteristics of feral or domestic hogs. Piglets are usually striped until about four months of age. Wild hogs have 44 teeth, including four continually growing tusks. The upper tusks rub against the lower, sharpening the edges.

◆ **STATUS & HABITAT**—The European wild hog is not native to North America. National Park Service policy states that control or eradication of non-native (exotic) species will be undertaken whenever such species threaten protection and interpretation of resources being preserved. Wild hogs were accidentally introduced into the park in the late 1940s after they escaped from a private hunting preserve in western North Carolina. They are destructive to both the natural and cultural resources of the park. Rooting disrupts plant communities and alters habitats of small animals. It also damages cultural resources such as old home sites and cemeteries. Wild hogs prey on native species and compete for important foods, especially acorns; they also carry diseases and parasites that affect other wildlife, livestock, and people.

Since 1959, the park has used livetrapping and shooting to remove over 11,000 wild hogs. During the late 1970s and early 1980s it is believed that nearly 3,000 hogs lived in the park. Since the mid 1990s, park biologists believe the annual peak for the hog population is 400 - 600. Although wild hogs have been known to be aggressive, only one minor human injury has been documented in the park, when a young boy came between a sow and her piglets.

Wild hogs eat just about anything: fungi, leaves, roots, bulbs, tubers, fruits, nuts, snails, salamanders, earthworms, reptiles, young birds, eggs, small mammals, and carrion. Wild hogs are found at all elevations in the park. However, their densities change seasonally. Wild hogs wallow in mud to keep cool and rid themselves of parasites. Their feeding activity is mainly nocturnal.

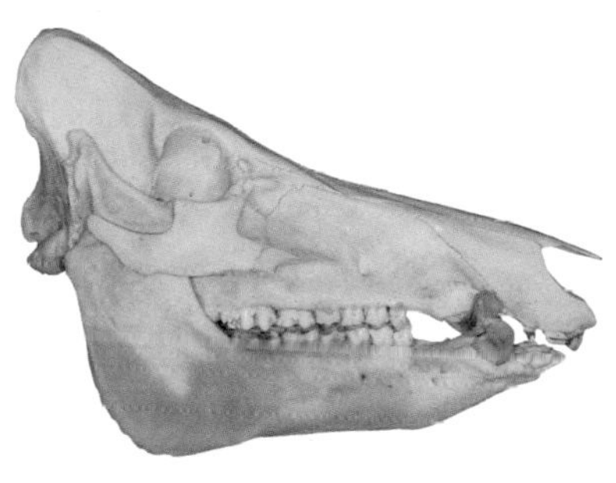

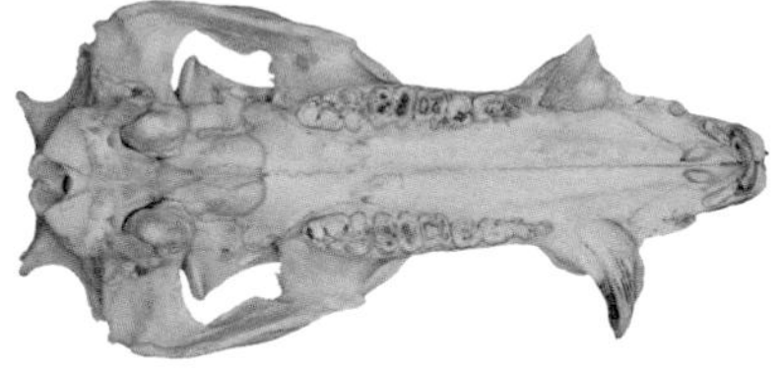

They reproduce faster than any other large wild mammal in North America. Females are capable of breeding at 8 - 10 months of age, can have two litters a year and average three to 12 piglets per litter. Except for the breeding season, mature male wild hogs are typically solitary. Major predators of wild hogs include black bears, bobcats, and coyotes.

ELK

Bill Lea

Cervus elaphus
Reintroduced

Head and body
72" - 105" length
(180 - 250 mm)

shoulder
48" - 60" height
(120 - 150 mm)

250 - 800 lbs
(110 - 360 kg)

ELEVATION

The elk or wapiti (a Shawnee name meaning "white rump") is the second largest species of deer in the world. Its upper body is brown and the under parts are paler. Elk also have a prominent pale-colored patch on the rump. Calves are spotted until about three months of age. Like other members of the deer family, male elk (bulls) have antlers, whereas females (cows) only rarely do. Antlers are appendages of the skull that begin to grow early in the summer. During this time, antlers have a rich blood supply, are soft and covered with fine hairs referred to as velvet, and can grow an inch per day. By late summer, the blood supply recedes and the velvety hair dries, loosens, and is rubbed off.

◆ **STATUS & HABITAT**—Historically, elk were found throughout the southern Appalachian Mountains. However, due to excessive hunting and loss of habitat, elk were eliminated from North Carolina by the late 1700s and Tennessee by the mid 1800s. The eastern elk subspecies (*Cervus elaphus canadensis*) is extinct. National Park Service policy encourages reintrodution of extirpated species when feasible. In 2001 and 2002, 52 elk (*Cervus elaphus manitobensis*) were released in Cataloochee Valley as part of an experiment to explore the feasibility of reestablishing this species into the park.

Elk live in a variety of habitats. They are primarily grazers, feeding largely on grasses, forbs, and sedges, but they will also eat acorns and browse on shrubs and deciduous trees. Places to view elk in the Smokies include Cataloochee Valley and Oconaluftee.

Elk are primarily found in the western United States and Canada.

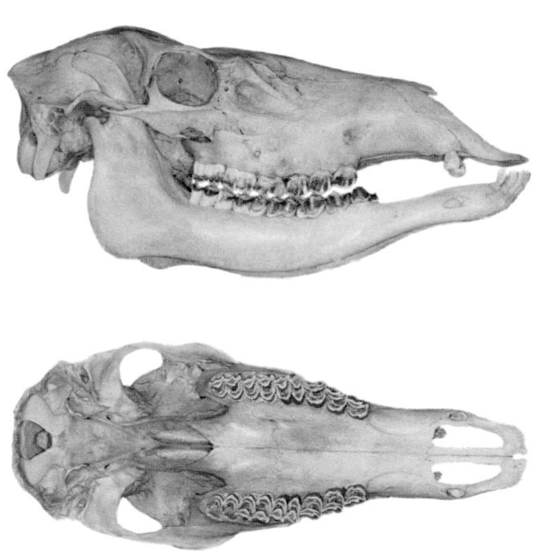

Free ranging populations in the eastern U.S. are found in Kentucky, Arkansas, Michigan, Pennsylvania, North Carolina, and Tennessee. The current North American elk population is about one million, which is only about ten percent of their estimated population before European settlers arrived. The largest elk herd east of the Mississippi River is found in southeastern Kentucky where nearly 6,000 elk live.

Female elk attain sexual maturity at about 28 months. The peak elk breeding season or "rut" is usually from late September to early October. During the rut, bulls produce a high pitched bugle call to attract females. The older, more powerful bulls drive off the younger or less dominant bulls and will form harems of several cows each. Females usually birth a single calf in June or July. Black bears and coyotes are the primary predators of newborn calves.

Bill Lea

Odocoileus virginianus

60″ - 80″
(137 - 183 mm)
30″- 42″ shoulder height
(76 - 107 mm)

75 - 250 lbs
(34 - 113 kg)

Bill Lea

The white-tailed deer takes its name from the white hair on the underside and edges of its tail. When frightened, the deer raises its tail, communicating danger to other deer. Newborn fawns are reddish brown with white spots, camouflaging them from predators. During summer, adults have a reddish brown color. During fall, both fawns and adults replace summer hair with a brownish-gray coat.

In addition to their white tails, white-tailed deer have white bellies and white hair under their chin and around their eyes and muzzle. Males (bucks) have antlers they shed in late winter. The deer breeding season or "rut" is from October into January. In the park, females usually do not mate until their second year; however, in areas with abundant and high-quality food they may breed late in their first year. Fawns are born from May through August with the peak from June through mid July. Females in the park usually give birth to only one fawn that weighs about six pounds (2.7 kg), but in higher-quality habitats, they may have twins or even triplets.

◆ **STATUS & HABITAT**—White-tailed deer occur throughout the park but their density is highest in Cades Cove, a historical area. In the past, the cultural landscape and open vistas of Cades Cove were maintained through haying and cattle grazing. Deer population surveys in the 1970s and early 1980s showed deer densities that appeared high in relation to the available habitat. During these times, a viral disease was responsible for high deer mortality and habitat degradation was noted. However, in recent years surveys have indicated an apparent decline in the size of the Cades Cove deer herd. Research findings suggest the animals are somewhat healthier. Although the

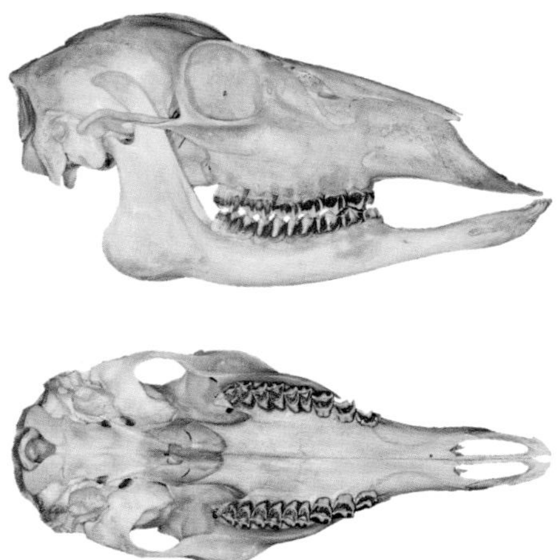

Bill Lea

Bill Lea

exact reason for the herd's population decline is unknown, predators may play an important role. Annually, visitors and park employees observe predators feeding on deer fawns. The major predators of deer in the park are black bear, coyote, and bobcat.

White-tailed deer are primarily browsers but live in a variety of habitats including farmlands, brushy areas, forests, and suburbs. Their diet includes twigs, buds, shrubs, fungi, acorns, grasses, and herbs.

Following European settlement, white-tailed deer were hunted extensively and by 1900 were extirpated from much of their range. However, through regulations, management, and environmental changes, deer numbers and distribution have increased significantly. Today, some estimates of white-tailed deer numbers in the United States exceed 30 million animals. In the park, deer populations appear to be more in balance with available habitat in part due to a healthy population of predators.

American Bison

© Dwight Kuhn

Bison bison
Extirpated

130″ - 180″ Head & body
(270 - 410 mm)
60″ - 71″ shoulder height
(150 - 180 mm)

690 - 1,970 lbs
(315 - 900 kg)
Males generally larger than females.

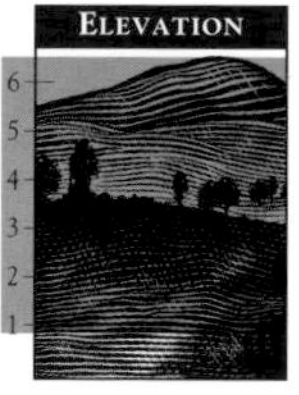

American bison or buffalo belong to the same family as cattle, sheep, and goats. Both sexes have short, curved horns that are never shed. There are two North American subspecies, the plains bison (*Bison bison bison*), distinguished by its flat back, and the wood bison (*Bison bison athabascae*), distinguished by its large humped back. During summer, bison have a lighter brown coat; during winter it turns a shaggy, dark brown. Bison are mature at three years and breeding occurs in August and September. Bulls maintain a small harem of females for mating. A newborn calf weighs 45 - 50 pounds. Calves have a light brown coat that darkens when it matures. On rare occasions calves may be white, but they are not albinos. Native Americans consider the white buffalo sacred.

◆ **STATUS & HABITAT**—The American bison is traditionally associated with the prairies, but it also inhabited mountainous areas and open forest, including the Smokies. There were once an estimated 50,000,000 buffalo in North America. Some Native American tribes depended on hunting these animals. They used bison in several ways, including meat for food, skin for clothing and shelter, sinew for thread and rope, hooves for glue and tools, and droppings as fuel. However, as European settlers arrived, bison were hunted commercially as well as for subsistence. By the early 20th century, bison had been eliminated from lands east of the Mississippi River, so little is known about them. It is estimated that bison were eliminated from the Great Smoky Mountains in the late 18th century. By 1890, fewer than 1,000 bison could be found in North America.

Bison feed mostly on grasses, but they will eat some browse.

The current American bison herd is estimated at 350,000, with free-ranging herds limited to a few areas in the western U.S. and Canada. Although National Park Service policy encourages the reintroduction of extirpated species, currently bison are not being considered for reintroduction to the Smokies.

GLOSSARY

ARBOREAL: Behavior associated with activity in trees.

AUDITORY BULLA: Typically a rounded series of bones that covers the middle and inner ear region of mammal skulls. Located as two prominent rounded and elevated areas at the bottom of the skull.

CALCAR: A cartilaginous projection from the ankle that supports the tail membrane of a bat.

CANINE: A tooth posterior to the incisors and anterior to the premolars that is usually elongated and single cusped. Well developed in carnivores.

CARNASSIALS: Found in carnivores and consists of the last upper premolar and the first lower molar. These teeth function as shearing blades on each side of the jaw.

CARPALS: The bones of the wrist.

CAUDAL: Pertaining to the tail.

CHEEK TEETH: The premolars and the molars.

CREPUSCULAR: Active at dawn and dusk.

CURSORIAL: Adapted for running.

DELAYED IMPLANTATION: Period during which development of a fertilized egg is suspended at an early phase (blastocyst stage) and implantation in the uterine wall is delayed. Common among members of the *Mustelidae* family.

DENTARY: The bone making up one half of the lower jaw.

DIASTEMA: A space between teeth.

DIURNAL: Activity restricted to daylight hours.

ECHOLOCATION: The process of locating distant objects by means of sound waves reflected back to the emitter.

FENESTRATED: Area of skull with light, lattice like bone structure.

FORAMEN: An opening or passage through a bone, which typically transmits a nerve or blood vessel.

FOSSORIAL: Behavior pertaining to digging and movements underground.

HALLUX: The large or "big" toe of the hind foot.

HIBERNACULUM: A shelter occupied by a hibernating animal.

INCISOR: Tooth anterior to the canines and rooted in the premaxillary bone (upper jaw) and in the lower jaw (dentary bones).

KARST: A limestone region with sinks, underground streams, and caverns.

MANDIBULAR FOSSA: The hinge point of the lower jaw (mandible) on the cranium.

MANUS: The forefoot or hand.

MESIC: Habitats that have moderate rainfall and humidity.

MIDDEN: A refuse or collection area in or around the nesting area of an individual.

MOLAR: Cheek teeth posterior to the premolars and found only in the adult. No deciduous or "baby" teeth prior to the eruption of the molars.

NEONATE: Newborn animal.

NOCTURNAL: Activity mainly at night.

PATAGIUM: A thin membrane that extends from the front limbs to the hind limbs in flying squirrels and functions as a gliding membrane.

PELAGE: The hairy covering of a mammal.

PES: The hind foot.

PINNA: The external ear flap that directs sound into the external auditory meatus (canal).

POLLEX: The "thumb."

PREHENSILE: Usually refers to the tail; the ability to wrap around an object.

PREMOLAR: Cheek teeth that are located posterior to the canines and anterior to the molars.

PROCUMBENT: Refers to teeth that project forward.

RIPARIAN: Habitats along the banks of a waterway.

ROSTRUM: Mammal's snout.

SALTATORY: Locomotion by leaping or jumping activity.

SEMIFOSSORIAL: Adapted partially for a burrowing or underground digging life style.

SONOGRAM: An image produced by ultrasound.

TARSAL: Ankle bones.

TORPOR: A lowering of the body temperature and the metabolic rate that aids the individual in lowering energetic demands at night and during the colder months of the year.

TRAGUS: A flap of tissue extending from the lower border of the external ear pinnae of bats. Functions to direct the ultrasonic cries of the bats back into the ear for more precision in echolocation.

ULTRASOUND: Sound with frequencies above the range of human hearing.

UNICUSPID: Tooth composed of a single cusp such as the canine tooth. However, shrews also have unicuspid premolar teeth.

UROPATAGIUM: The flight membrane of bats that extends from the hind legs to the tail; may totally encompass the tail.

XERIC: Dry habitat.

ZYGOMATIC ARCH: The "cheek bone" of the human skull that forms an arch of bone on the side of the mammalian skull. Formed by the jugal and the squamosal bones. Site of attachment of the major jaw muscle, the masseter.

Species Index

Common and scientific names